C000065250

Teacher's Guide 2
Spelling Skills

Author: Sarah Snashall

William Collins' dream of knowledge for all began with the publication of his first book in 1819.

A self-educated mill worker, he not only enriched millions of lives, but also founded a flourishing publishing house. Today, staying true to this spirit, Collins books are packed with inspiration, innovation and practical expertise. They place you at the centre of a world of possibility and give you exactly what you need to explore it.

Collins. Freedom to teach.

Published by Collins
An imprint of HarperCollins*Publishers*
The News Building
1 London Bridge Street
London
SE1 9GF

Browse the complete Collins catalogue at
www.collins.co.uk

978-0-00-822309-0

British Library Cataloguing in Publication Data

A catalogue record for this publication is available from the British Library.

Publishing Director: Lee Newman
Publishing Manager: Helen Doran
Senior Editor: Hannah Dove
Project Manager: Emily Hooton
Author: Sarah Snashall
Development Editor: Jessica Marshall
Copy-editor: Tanya Solomons
Proofreader: Gaynor Spry
Cover design and artwork: Amparo Barrera and Ken Vail Graphic Design
Internal design concept: Amparo Barrera
Typesetter: Jouve India Private Ltd
Illustrations: Alberto Saichann (Beehive Illustration)
Production Controller: Rachel Weaver

Printed and bound by CPI Group (UK) Ltd, Croydon, CR0 4YY

Contents

About Treasure House

Treasure House is a comprehensive and flexible bank of books and online resources for teaching the English curriculum. The Treasure House series offers two different pathways: one covering each English strand discretely (Skills Focus Pathway) and one integrating texts and the strands to create a programme of study (Integrated English Pathway). This Teacher's Guide is part of the Skills Focus Pathway.

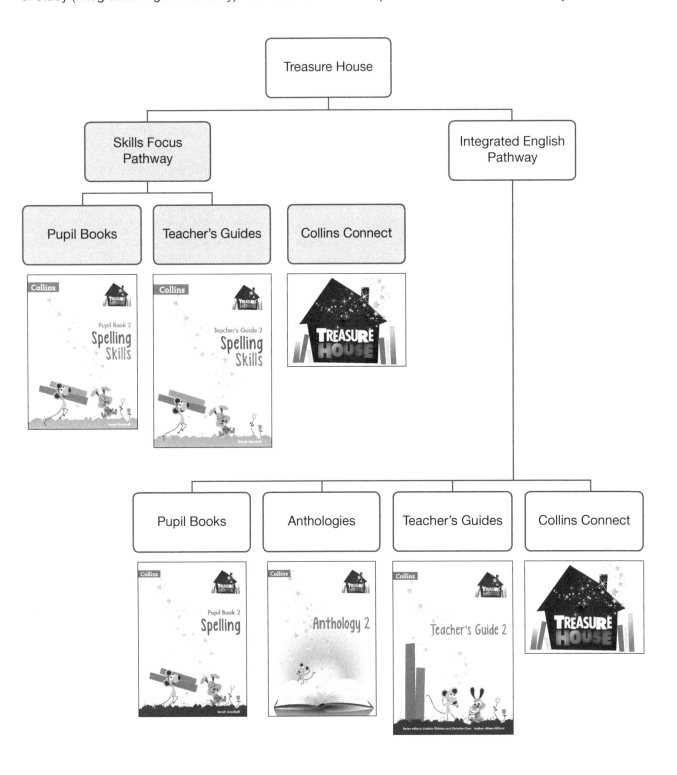

1. Skills Focus

The Skills Focus Pupil Books and Teacher's Guides for all four strands (Comprehension; Spelling; Composition; and Vocabulary, Grammar and Punctuation) allow you to teach each curriculum area in a targeted way. Each unit in the Pupil Book is mapped directly to the statutory requirements of the National Curriculum. Each Teacher's Guide provides step-by-step instructions to guide you through the Pupil Book activities and digital Collins Connect resources for each competency. With a clear focus on skills and clearly-listed curriculum objectives you can select the appropriate resources to support your lessons.

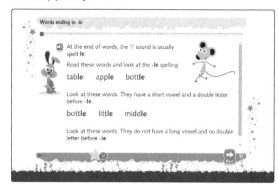

2. Integrated English

Alternatively, the Integrated English pathway offers a complete programme of genre-based teaching sequences. There is one Teacher's Guide and one Anthology for each year group. Each Teacher's Guide provides 15 teaching sequences focused on different genres of text such as fairy tales, letters and newspaper articles. The Anthologies contain the classic texts, fiction, non-fiction and poetry required for each sequence. Each sequence also weaves together all four dimensions of the National Curriculum for English – Comprehension; Spelling; Composition; and Vocabulary, Grammar and Punctuation – into a complete English programme. The Pupil Books and Collins Connect provide targeted explanation of key points and practice activities organised by strand. This programme provides 30 weeks of teaching inspiration.

Other components

Handwriting Books, Handwriting Workbooks, Word Books and the online digital resources on Collins Connect are suitable for use with both pathways.

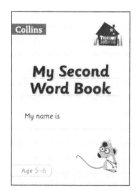

Treasure House Skills Focus Teacher's Guides

Year	Comprehension	Composition	Vocabulary, Grammar and Punctuation	Spelling
1	978-0-00-822290-1	978-0-00-822302-1	978-0-00-822296-3	978-0-00-822308-3
2	978-0-00-822291-8	978-0-00-822303-8	978-0-00-822297-0	978-0-00-822309-0
3	978-0-00-822292-5	978-0-00-822304-5	978-0-00-822298-7	978-0-00-822310-6
4	978-0-00-822293-2	978-0-00-822305-2	978-0-00-822299-4	978-0-00-822311-3
5	978-0-00-822294-9	978-0-00-822306-9	978-0-00-822300-7	978-0-00-822312-0
6	978-0-00-822295-6	978-0-00-822307-6	978-0-00-822301-4	978-0-00-822313-7

Inside the Skills Focus Teacher's Guides

The teaching notes in each unit of the Teacher's Guide provide you with subject information or background, a range of whole class and differentiated activities including photocopiable resource sheets and links to the Pupil Book and the online Collins Connect activities.

Each **Overview** provides clear objectives for each lesson tied into the new curriculum, links to the other relevant components and a list of any additional resources required.

Teaching overview introduces each spelling rule and provides a list of key words that follow the rule that are useful to the age group.

Support, embed & challenge supports a mastery approach with activities provided at three levels.

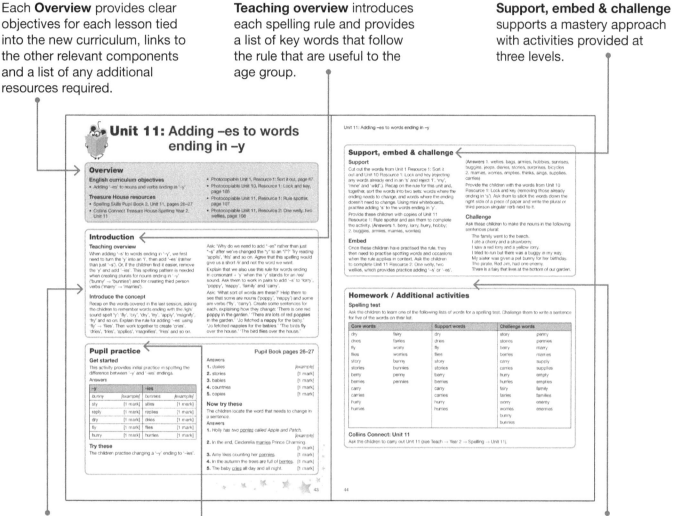

Introduce the concept provides 5–10 minutes of preliminary discussion points or class/group activities to get the pupils engaged in the lesson focus and set out any essential prior learning.

Pupil practice gives guidance and the answers to each of the three sections in the Pupil Book: *Get started*, *Try these* and *Now try these*.

Homework / Additional activities lists ideas for classroom or homework activities, and relevant activities from Collins Connect.

Two photocopiable **resource** worksheets per unit provide extra practice of the specific lesson concept. They are designed to be used with the activities in support, embed or challenge sections.

Treasure House Skills Focus Pupil Books

There are four Skills Focus Pupil Books for each year group, based on the four dimensions of the National Curriculum for English: Comprehension; Spelling; Composition; and Vocabulary, Grammar and Punctuation. The Pupil Books provide a child-friendly introduction to each subject and a range of initial activities for independent pupil-led learning. A Review unit for each term assesses pupils' progress.

Year	Comprehension	Composition	Vocabulary, Grammar and Punctuation	Spelling
1	978-0-00-823634-2	978-0-00-823646-5	978-0-00-823640-3	978-0-00-823652-6
2	978-0-00-823635-9	978-0-00-823647-2	978-0-00-823641-0	978-0-00-823653-3
3	978-0-00-823636-6	978-0-00-823648-9	978-0-00-823642-7	978-0-00-823654-0
4	978-0-00-823637-3	978-0-00-823649-6	978-0-00-823643-4	978-0-00-823655-7
5	978-0-00-823638-0	978-0-00-823650-2	978-0-00-823644-1	978-0-00-823656-4
6	978-0-00-823639-7	978-0-00-823651-9	978-0-00-823645-8	978-0-00-823657-1

Inside the Skills Focus Pupil Books

Comprehension

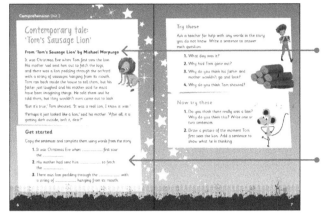

Includes high-quality text extracts covering poetry, prose, traditional tales, playscripts and non-fiction.

Pupils retrieve and record information, learn to draw inferences from texts and increase their familiarity with a wide range of literary genres.

Composition

Includes high-quality, annotated text extracts as models for different types of writing.

Children learn how to write effectively and for a purpose.

Vocabulary, Grammar and Punctuation

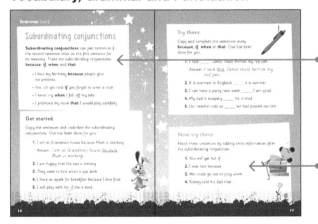

Develops children's knowledge and understanding of grammar and punctuation skills.

A rule is introduced and explained. Children are given lots of opportunities to practise using it.

Spelling

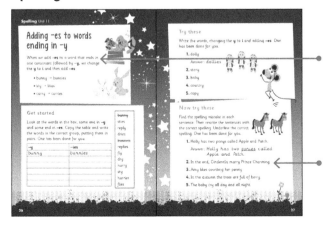

Spelling rules are introduced and explained.

Practice is provided for spotting and using the spelling rules, correcting misspelt words and using the words in context.

Treasure House on Collins Connect

Digital resources for Treasure House are available on Collins Connect which provides a wealth of interactive activities. Treasure House is organised into six core areas on Collins Connect:

- Comprehension
- Spelling
- Composition
- Vocabulary, Grammar and Punctuation
- The Reading Attic
- Teacher's Guides and Anthologies.

For most units in the Skills Focus Pupil Books, there is an accompanying Collins Connect unit focused on the same teaching objective. These fun, independent activities can be used for initial pupil-led learning, or for further practice using a different learning environment. Either way, with Collins Connect, you have a wealth of questions to help children embed their learning.

Treasure House on Collins Connect is available via subscription at connect.collins.co.uk

Features of Treasure House on Collins Connect

The digital resources enhance children's comprehension, spelling, composition, and vocabulary, grammar, punctuation skills through providing:

- a bank of varied and engaging interactive activities so children can practise their skills independently
- audio support to help children access the texts and activities
- auto-mark functionality so children receive instant feedback and have the opportunity to repeat tasks.

Teachers benefit from useful resources and time-saving tools including:

- teacher-facing materials such as audio and explanations for front-of-class teaching or pupil-led learning
- lesson starter videos for some Composition units
- downloadable teaching notes for all online activities
- downloadable teaching notes for Skills Focus and Integrated English pathways
- the option to assign homework activities to your classes
- class records to monitor progress.

Comprehension

- Includes high-quality text extracts covering poetry, prose, traditional tales, playscripts and non-fiction.
- Audio function supports children to access the text and the activities

Composition

- Activities support children to develop and build more sophisticated sentence structures.
- Every unit ends with a longer piece of writing that can be submitted to the teacher for marking.

Vocabulary, Grammar and Punctuation

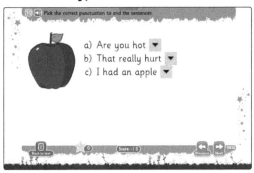

- Fun, practical activities develop children's knowledge and understanding of grammar and punctuation skills.
- Each skill is reinforced with a huge, varied bank of practice questions.

Spelling

- Fun, practical activities develop children's knowledge and understanding of each spelling rule.
- Each rule is reinforced with a huge, varied bank of practice questions.
- Children spell words using an audio prompt, write their own sentences and practise spelling using Look Say Cover Write Check.

Reading Attic

- Children's love of reading is nurtured with texts from exciting children's authors including Micheal Bond, David Walliams and Micheal Morpurgo.
- Lesson sequences accompany the texts, with drama opportunities and creative strategies for engaging children with key themes, characters and plots.
- Whole-book projects encourage reading for pleasure.

Treasure House Digital Teacher's Guides and Anthologies

The teaching sequences and anthology texts for each year group are included as a flexible bank of resources.

The teaching notes for each skill strand and year group are also included on Collins Connect.

Support, embed and challenge

Treasure House provides comprehensive, detailed differentiation at three levels to ensure that all children are able to access achievement. It is important that children master the basic skills before they go further in their learning. Children may make progress towards the standard at different speeds, with some not reaching it until the very end of the year.

In the Teacher's Guide, Support, Embed and Challenge sections allow teachers to keep the whole class focussed with no child left behind. Two photocopiable resources per unit offer additional material linked to the Support, Embed or Challenge sections.

Support

The Support section in Spelling offers scaffolded activities (suitable for use in small groups with adult support) that will help learners who have not yet grasped the specific spelling rule. These activities use fewer or more straightforward words and are usually supported with a photocopiable resource sheet.

If you have a teaching assistant, you may wish to ask him or her to help children work through these activities. You might then ask children who have completed these activities to progress to other more challenging tasks found in the Embed or Challenge sections – or you may decide more practice of the basics is required. Collins Connect can provide further activities.

Embed

The Embed section includes activities to embed learning and is aimed at those who children who are working at the expected standard. It ensures that learners have understood key teaching objectives for the age-group. These activities could be used by the whole class or groups, and most are appropriate for both teacher-led and independent work.

In Spelling, the Embed section provides activities to embed learning following the whole class introduction and is aimed at those who children who are working at the expected standard. After the children have learnt each rule, this section provides a range of fun small group games and activities to help the children (working without an adult) to learn words with the spelling pattern. A photocopiable resource sheet is provided for each unit.

Challenge

The Challenge section provides additional tasks, questions or activities that will push children who have mastered the spelling rule without difficulty. This keeps children motivated and allows them to gain a greater depth of understanding. You may wish to give these activities to fast finishers to work through independently.

Children who are working above the expected level may progress to focusing on the spelling of less common, longer words or they might investigate exceptions to the rule and creating posters for the class. Challenge activities are provided to stretch the children's understanding of the rule or to enhance vocabulary work.

Differentiated spelling lists

In the Homework section, you will find word lists for spelling tests. There is a standard list and there are also two targeted lists; *Support words* list is suitable for children who are struggling with the concept. The list is shorter and contains words that are more common, shorter, simpler or more regular. The *Challenge words* list is a longer list often with more challenging words, suitable for children who have grasped the rule/concept.

Differentiated weekly spelling lists are provided for each unit and details of any matching Collins Connect units.

Assessment

Teacher's Guide

There are opportunities for assessment throughout the Treasure House series. The teaching notes in the Skills Focus Teacher's Guides offer ideas for questions, informal assessment and spelling tests.

Pupil Book Review units

Each Pupil Book has three Review units designed as a quick formative assessment tool for the end of each term. Questions assess the work that has been covered over the previous units. These review units will provide you with an informal way of measuring your pupils' progress. You may wish to use these as Assessment *for* Learning to help you and your pupils to understand where they are in their learning journey.

The Review units in the Spelling and Vocabulary, Grammar and Punctuation Pupil Books, include questions testing rules taught in preceding units. By mixing questions on different unit topics within exercises, children can show understanding of multiple rules and patterns.

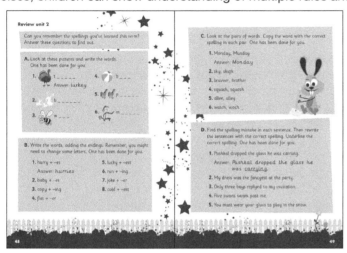

Assessment in Collins Connect

Activities on Collins Connect can also be used for effective assessment. Activities with auto-marking mean that if children answer incorrectly, they can make another attempt helping them to analyse their own work for mistakes. Homework activities can also be assigned to classes through Collins Connect. At the end of activities, children can select a smiley face to indicate how they found the task giving you useful feedback on any gaps in knowledge.

Class records on Collins Connect allow you to get an overview of children's progress with several features. You can choose to view records by unit, pupil or strand. By viewing detailed scores, you can view pupils' scores question by question in a clear table-format to help you establish areas where there might be particular strengths and weaknesses both class-wide and for individuals.

If you wish, you can also set mastery judgements (mastery achieved and exceeded, mastery achieved, mastery not yet achieved) to help see where your children need more help.

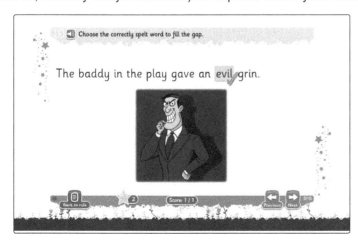

Support with teaching spelling

Trying to teach and understand the vagaries of English spelling is enough to drive the most patient of us to distraction. Think on those lucky countries such as Poland with phonetically consistent spelling. However, many words in English are phonetic and this should remain our starting point for all unknown words, with the children becoming increasingly confident in their knowledge of the spelling options for each sound.

The National Curriculum in England encourages us to teach the rules and patterns that are associated with each spelling cluster. In some cases these rules are easy to absorb, for example 'i before c except after c'. Others remain more elusive, such as hearing the stress in a word before deciding whether to double the last letter or not. You will have to judge for yourself when the rule is going to aid children in their learning and when they would be better off just learning the rules. (There are times when you have just got your head around a complicated rule to discover that there are only five suitable words for your class.) However, a knowledge and understanding of rules that do apply will provide children with the skills to manipulate language and root words, such as by adding suffixes and prefixes, to create specific vocabulary for their writing. This in turn will increase their confidence in writing. Teaching children to understand the relationship between words, such as 'grace' and 'gracious' not only develops their vocabulary but aids their spelling too.

This spelling scheme by its nature focuses on learning words as a separate activity: games, spelling tests and sometimes sentences. But, of course, this is only part of the picture. Children who read a lot will naturally absorb spelling as they regularly come across common words. Children who write a lot will naturally practise words that they want to use. Learning to spell words is only of any use if you use them at some point. Therefore, the activities in this scheme can only form part of the picture.

Weekly spelling test

The weekly spelling test remains crucial to learning the huge bank of words needed by the end of primary school. Spelling lists are provided in this scheme, but you may want to add or remove words depending on the abilities of the children in your class and the number of words you feel it is appropriate for them to learn. You will need to strike a balance between developing their vocabulary and providing useful words for them to learn.

You may also wish to enhance their spelling lists with words that they have spelt wrong during their writing tasks, or specific topic-led vocabulary.

Spelling games

The activities in this scheme aim to be fun and game-like. Many of the activities in the book are introduced for use with a particular set of words but many can be adapted for any word list you are practising (they mainly involve creating a set of word cards):

Pairs: Create two sets of word cards for the words you are practising and use them to play a game of pairs. Alternatively, use words with and without suffixes and prefixes or words related in other ways (such as different spellings for the same sound or homophones) and challenge the children to find the two associated words.

Simon's Game: When asking the children to learn a specific set of words, such as words with 'c' for /s/, ask pairs of children to remember the words on the list.

Pick a card: the children place a set of word cards between them and take turns to draw a card and test their partner or the next child around the table.

Hangman: Tell the children to play Hangman using words from previous two or three weeks' spellings. This encourages an attention to the specific letters and can be particularly useful when practising words with silent letters.

Bingo: Create Bingo cards for the words you are studying (ensuring each card has a slightly different word selection). When playing Bingo, the children spend the session staring at the words on their sheet – a useful way to add the word to the subconscious.

Game board: Create a simple board game where the children roll a dice to progress along a series of squares some of which require them to spell one of the words from the list (when someone draws a card and reads it to them). The board can be reused with any new set of words cards.

Differentiation

The lesson plans in this book provide three levels of differentiation. However, you may wish to provide further practice (Support or Challenge) at Years 3 and 4 or Years 5 and 6 by supplying the relevant children with the book for the other year group, as the words covered are the same. You may also wish to recap on words from earlier years for those children whose spelling needs further help.

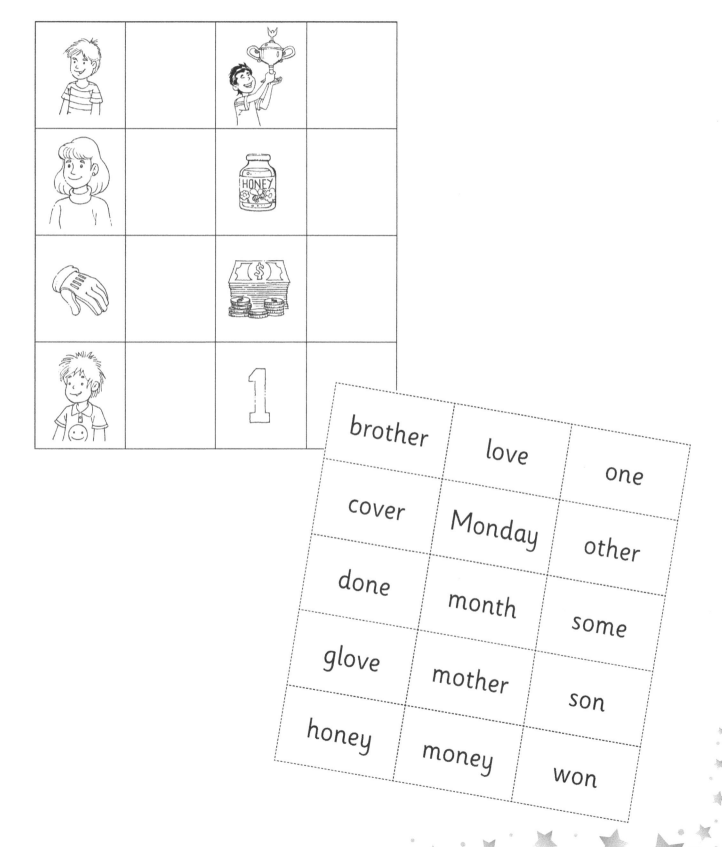

Delivering the 2014 National Curriculum for English

Unit	Title	Treasure House resources	Collins Connect	English Programme of Study	English Grammar, Punctuation and Spelling Test code

1	Words ending in –ge	• Spelling Skills Pupil Book 2, Unit 1, pages 4–5
		• Spelling Skills Teacher's Guide 2
		  – Unit 1, pages 22–23
		  – Photocopiable Unit 1, Resource 1: Sort it out, page 87
		  – Photocopiable Unit 1, Resource 2: Lunge for the sponge, page 88
			Treasure House Spelling Year 2, Unit 1	The /dʒ/ sound spelt as ge and dge at the end of words	S14

2	Words ending in –dge	• Spelling Skills Pupil Book 2, Unit 2, pages 6–7
		• Spelling Skills Teacher's Guide 2
		  – Unit 2, pages 24–25
		  – Photocopiable Unit 2, Resource 1: Circle time, page 89
		  – Photocopiable Unit 2, Resource 2: Bage or badge? page 90
			Treasure House Spelling Year 2, Unit 2	The /dʒ/ sound spelt as ge and dge at the end of words	S14

3	Spelling c before e, i and y	• Spelling Skills Pupil Book 2, Unit 3, pages 8–9
		• Spelling Skills Teacher's Guide 2
		  – Unit 3, pages 26–27
		  – Photocopiable Unit 3, Resource 1: Rice and mice, page 91
		  – Photocopiable Unit 3, Resource 2: Spelling spotter, page 92
			Treasure House Spelling Year 2, Unit 3	The /s/ sound spelt c before e, i and y	S15

4	Words beginning with kn– and gn–	• Spelling Skills Pupil Book 2, Unit 4, pages 10–11
		• Spelling Skills Teacher's Guide 2
		  – Unit 4, pages 28–29
		  – Photocopiable Unit 4, Resource 1: Four in a row, page 93
		  – Photocopiable Unit 4, Resource 2: Do you know which no? page 94
			Treasure House Spelling Year 2, Unit 4	The /n/ sound spelt kn and gn at the beginning of words	S16

5	Words beginning wr–	• Spelling Skills Pupil Book 2, Unit 5, pages 12–13
		• Spelling Skills Teacher's Guide 2
		  – Unit 5, pages 30–31
		  – Photocopiable Unit 5, Resource 1: Write and wrong, page 95
		  – Photocopiable Unit 5, Resource 2: Wriggles and wrinkles, page 96
			Treasure House Spelling Year 2, Unit 5	The /r/ sound spelt wr at the beginning of words	S17

6	Words ending in –le	• Spelling Skills Pupil Book 2, Unit 6, pages 14–15
		• Spelling Skills Teacher's Guide 2
		  – Unit 6, pages 32–33
		  – Photocopiable Unit 6, Resource 1: Apple on the table, page 97
		  – Photocopiable Unit 6, Resource 2: At the fair, page 98
			Treasure House Spelling Year 2, Unit 6	The /l/ or /əl/ sound spelt –le at the end of words	S18

Unit	Title	Treasure House resources	Collins Connect	English Programme of Study	English Grammar, Punctuation and Spelling Test code

7	Words ending in –el	• Spelling Skills Pupil Book 2, Unit 7, pages 16–17
		• Spelling Skills Teacher's Guide 2
		  – Unit 7, pages 34–35
		  – Photocopiable Unit 7, Resource 1: Word match, page 99
		  – Photocopiable Unit 7, Resource 2: Choosing –le and –el, page 100
			Treasure House Spelling Year 2, Unit 7	The /l/ or /əl/ sound spelt –el at the end of words	S19

8	Words ending in –al	• Spelling Skills Pupil Book 2, Unit 8, pages 18–19
		• Spelling Skills Teacher's Guide 2
		  – Unit 8, pages 36–37
		  – Photocopiable Unit 8, Resource 1: Green crystal, page 101
		  – Photocopiable Unit 8, Resource 2: Spelling trios, page 102
			Treasure House Spelling Year 2, Unit 8	The /l/ or /əl/ sound spelt –al at the end of words	S20

9	Words ending in –il	• Spelling Skills Pupil Book 2, Unit 9, pages 20–21
		• Spelling Skills Teacher's Guide 2
		  – Unit 9, pages 38–39
		  – Photocopiable Unit 6, Resource 2: At the fair, page 98
		  – Photocopiable Unit 7, Resource 1: Word match, page 99
		  – Photocopiable Unit 9, Resource 1: Fossil, gerbil, basil, page 103
		  – Photocopiable Unit 9, Resource 2: Memory test, page 104
			Treasure House Spelling Year 2, Unit 9	Words ending –il	S21

10	Words ending in –y	• Spelling Skills Pupil Book 2, Unit 10, pages 22–23
		• Spelling Skills Teacher's Guide 2
		  – Unit 10, pages 40–41
		  – Photocopiable Unit 10, Resource 1: Lock and key, page 105
		  – Photocopiable Unit 10, Resource 2: Crossword, page 106
			Treasure House Spelling Year 2, Unit 10	The /aɪ/ sound spelt –y at the end of words	S22

11	Adding –es to words ending in –y	• Spelling Skills Pupil Book 2, Unit 11, pages 26–27
		• Spelling Skills Teacher's Guide 2
		  – Unit 11, pages 43–44
		  – Photocopiable Unit 1, Resource 1: Sort it out, page 87
		  – Photocopiable Unit 10, Resource 1: Lock and key, page 105
		  – Photocopiable Unit 11, Resource 1: Rule spotter, page 107
		  – Photocopiable Unit 11, Resource 2: One welly, two wellies, page 108
			Treasure House Spelling Year 2, Unit 11	Adding –es to nouns and verbs ending in –y	S23
					G6.3

Unit	Title	Treasure House resources	Collins Connect	English Programme of Study	English Grammar, Punctuation and Spelling Test code

12	Adding –ed to words ending in –y	• Spelling Skills Pupil Book 2, Unit 12, pages 28–29
		• Spelling Skills Teacher's Guide 2
		  – Unit 12, pages 45–46
		  – Photocopiable Unit 12, Resource 1: Hurried word cards, page 109
		  – Photocopiable Unit 12, Resource 2: A hurried word search, page 110
			Treasure House Spelling Year 2, Unit 12	Adding –ed, –ing, –er and –est to a root word ending in –y with a consonant before it	S24

13	Adding –er or –est to root words ending in –y	• Spelling Skills Pupil Book 2, Unit 13, pages 30–31
		• Spelling Skills Teacher's Guide 2
		  – Unit 13, pages 47–48
		  – Photocopiable Unit 13, Resource 1: Funnier word cards, page 111
		  – Photocopiable Unit 13, Resource 2: Silliest sentences, page 112
			Treasure House Spelling Year 2, Unit 13	Adding –ed, –ing, –er and –est to a root word ending in –y with a consonant before it	S24

14	Adding –ing to root words ending in –y	• Spelling Skills Pupil Book 2, Unit 14, pages 32–33
		• Spelling Skills Teacher's Guide 2
		  – Unit 14, pages 49–50
		  – Photocopiable Unit 14, Resource 1: Multiply endings, page 113
		  – Photocopiable Unit 14, Resource 2: Tons of sums, page 114
			Treasure House Spelling Year 2, Unit 14	Adding –ed, –ing, –er and –est to a root word ending in –y with a consonant before it	S24

15	Adding new endings to root words ending in –e	• Spelling Skills Pupil Book 2, Unit 15, pages 34–35
		• Spelling Skills Teacher's Guide 2
		  – Unit 15, pages 51–52
		  – Photocopiable Unit 15, Resource 1: Working hard, page 115
		  – Photocopiable Unit 15, Resource 2: Dance, dancer, dancing, page 116
			Treasure House Spelling Year 2, Unit 15	Adding the endings –ing, –ed, –er, –est and –y to words ending in –e with a consonant before it	S25

16	Adding new endings to one-syllable words with short vowel sounds	• Spelling Skills Pupil Book 2, Unit 16, pages 36–37
		• Spelling Skills Teacher's Guide 2
		  – Unit 16, pages 53–54
		  – Photocopiable Unit 16, Resource 1: Double letters, page 117
		  – Photocopiable Unit 16, Resource 2: Running on a sunny day, page 118
			Treasure House Spelling Year 2, Unit 16	Adding –ing, –ed, –er, –est and –y to words of one syllable ending in a single consonant letter after a single vowel letter	S26

Unit	Title	Treasure House resources	Collins Connect	English Programme of Study	English Grammar, Punctuation and Spelling Test code
17	Spelling words with al or all	• Spelling Skills Pupil Book 2, Unit 17, pages 38–39 • Spelling Skills Teacher's Guide 2 – Unit 17, pages 55–56 – Photocopiable Unit 17, Resource 1: Sort them all out, page 119 – Photocopiable Unit 17, Resource 2: Find them all, page 120	Treasure House Spelling Year 2, Unit 17	The /ɔː/ sound spelt a before l and ll	S27
18	The /u/ sound spelt o	• Spelling Skills Pupil Book 2, Unit 18, pages 40–41 • Spelling Skills Teacher's Guide 2 – Unit 18, pages 57–58 – Photocopiable Unit 18, Resource 1: Picture match, page 121 – Photocopiable Unit 18, Resource 2: Pairs, page 122	Treasure House Spelling Year 2, Unit 18	The /ʌ/ sound spelt o	S28
19	The /ee/ sound spelt –ey	• Spelling Skills Pupil Book 2, Unit 19, pages 42–43 • Spelling Skills Teacher's Guide 2 – Unit 19, pages 59–60 – Photocopiable Unit 19, Resource 1: Finish it off, page 123 – Photocopiable Unit 19, Resource 2: Plural mix up, page 124	Treasure House Spelling Year 2, Unit 19	The /iː/ sound spelt –ey	S29
20	The /o/ sound spelt a after w and qu	• Spelling Skills Pupil Book 2, Unit 20, pages 44–45 • Spelling Skills Teacher's Guide 2 – Unit 20, pages 61–62 – Photocopiable Unit 20, Resource 1: Match the word, page 125 – Photocopiable Unit 20, Resource 2: Word duos, page 126	Treasure House Spelling Year 2, Unit 20	The /ɒ/ sound spelt a after w and qu	S30
21	The /er/ sound spelt or after w	• Spelling Skills Pupil Book 2, Unit 21, pages 46–47 • Spelling Skills Teacher's Guide 2 – Unit 21, pages 63–64 – Photocopiable Unit 21, Resource 1: /er/ sound word search, page 127 – Photocopiable Unit 21, Resource 2: Choose the spelling, page 128	Treasure House Spelling Year 2, Unit 21	The /ɜː/ sound spelt or after w	S31
22	The /or/ sound spelt ar after w	• Spelling Skills Pupil Book 2, Unit 22, pages 50–51 • Spelling Skills Teacher's Guide 2 – Unit 22, pages 66–67 – Photocopiable Unit 22, Resource 1: Towards awards, page 129 – Photocopiable Unit 22, Resource 2: Meaning match, page 130	Treasure House Spelling Year 2, Unit 22	The /ɔː/ sound spelt ar after w	S32

Unit	Title	Treasure House resources	Collins Connect	English Programme of Study	English Grammar, Punctuation and Spelling Test code

23	The /zh/ sound spelt s	• Spelling Skills Pupil Book 2, Unit 23, pages 52–53
		• Spelling Skills Teacher's Guide 2
		  – Unit 23, pages 68–69
		  – Photocopiable Unit 23, Resource 1: A little bit of treasure, page 131
		  – Photocopiable Unit 23, Resource 2: A difficult decision, page 132
			Treasure House Spelling Year 2, Unit 23	The /ʒ/ sound spelt s	S33

24	Adding the suffixes –ment, –ness, ful, –less and –ly (1)	• Spelling Skills Pupil Book 2, Unit 24, pages 54–55
		• Spelling Skills Teacher's Guide 2
		  – Unit 24, pages 70–71
		  – Photocopiable Unit 24, Resource 1: Add it on!, page 133
		  – Photocopiable Unit 24, Resource 2: Hopefully adding helpful suffixes, page 134
			Treasure House Spelling Year 2, Unit 24	The suffixes –ment, –ness, –ful, –less and –ly	S34
					G6.3

25	Adding the suffixes –ment, –ness, ful, –less and – ly (2)	• Spelling Skills Pupil Book 2, Unit 25, pages 56–57
		• Spelling Skills Teacher's Guide 2
		  – Unit 25, pages 72–73
		  – Photocopiable Unit 25, Resource 1: Lucky and luckily, page 135
		  – Photocopiable Unit 25, Resource 2: Heavily and angrily, page 136
			Treasure House Spelling Year 2, Unit 25	The suffixes –ment, –ness, –ful, –less and –ly	S34
					G6.3

26	Apostrophes for contractions	• Spelling Skills Pupil Book 2, Unit 26, pages 58–59
		• Spelling Skills Teacher's Guide 2
		  – Unit 26, pages 74–75
		  – Photocopiable Unit 26, Resource 1: Contraction pairs, page 137
		  – Photocopiable Unit 26, Resource 2: Pull it together, page 138
			Treasure House Spelling Year 2, Unit 26	Contractions	G5.8

27	Apostrophes to show possession	• Spelling Skills Pupil Book 2, Unit 27, pages 60–61
		• Spelling Skills Teacher's Guide 2
		  – Unit 27, pages 76–77
		  – Photocopiable Unit 27, Resource 1: Whose arm is this? page 139
		  – Photocopiable Unit 27, Resource 2: Wanted: missing apostrophe, page 140
			Treasure House Spelling Year 2, Unit 27	The possessive apostrophe (singular nouns)	G5.8

Unit	Title	Treasure House resources	Collins Connect	English Programme of Study	English Grammar, Punctuation and Spelling Test code
28	Words ending in –tion	• Spelling Skills Pupil Book 2, Unit 28, pages 62–63 • Spelling Skills Teacher's Guide 2 – Unit 28, pages 78–79 – Photocopiable Unit 28, Resource 1: Action at the station, page 141 – Photocopiable Unit 28, Resource 2: Wrong direction, page 142	Treasure House Spelling Year 2, Unit 28	Words ending in –tion	S35
29	Homophones (1)	• Spelling Skills Pupil Book 2, Unit 29, pages 64–65 • Spelling Skills Teacher's Guide 2 – Unit 29, pages 80–81 – Photocopiable Unit 29, Resource 1: Write it right, page 143 – Photocopiable Unit 29, Resource 2: Here, hear! page 144	Treasure House Spelling Year 2, Unit 29	Homophones and near-homophones	S36
30	Homophone and near homophones	• Spelling Skills Pupil Book 2, Unit 30, pages 66–67 • Spelling Skills Teacher's Guide 2 – Unit 30, pages 82–83 – Photocopiable Unit 30, Resource 1: Pairs of pears, page 145 – Photocopiable Unit 30, Resource 2: Definition match, page 146	Treasure House Spelling Year 2, Unit 30	Homophones and near-homophones	S36
31	Homophones (2)	• Spelling Skills Pupil Book 2, Unit 31, pages 68–69 • Spelling Skills Teacher's Guide 2 – Unit 31, pages 84–85 – Photocopiable Unit 31, Resource 1: Two many twos to remember!, page 147 – Photocopiable Unit 31, Resource 2: Definition mission, page 148	Treasure House Spelling Year 2, Unit 31	Homophones and near-homophones	S36

Unit 1: Words ending in –ge

Overview

English curriculum objectives

- The /j/ sound spelt as '–ge' and '–dge' at the end of words

Treasure House resources

- Spelling Skills Pupil Book 2, Unit 1, pages 4–5
- Collins Connect Treasure House Spelling Year 2, Unit 1

- Photocopiable Unit 1, Resource 1: Sort it out, page 87
- Photocopiable Unit 1, Resource 2: Lunge for the sponge, page 88

Additional resources

- Children's reading books

Introduction

Teaching overview

The /j/ sound can be spelt 'j', 'g', '–ge' and '–dge' depending on its position in a word. In Year 1, the children will have learned that a soft /j/ at the beginning of a word is usually spelt 'j'. Now, the children need to begin to choose correctly between '–ge' and '–dge' at the end of a word. They should learn that '–ge' is used: when the preceding vowel sound is long, such as in 'cage', 'huge', 'bilge' and 'change'; when a two-syllable word ends in an /idge/ sound, such as in 'cottage' and 'message' (apart from 'porridge', 'partridge', 'knowledge' and compound words ending '–bridge'); when the /j/ sound is preceded by an 'r' or an 'n'. For short words with a short vowel sound, the /j/ is spelt '–dge', for example 'bridge', 'fudge', 'badge'.

Introduce the concept

Ask the children, in pairs, to write five words on their mini whiteboards that have the /j/ sound, challenging more able children to write words that have the /j/ sound in the middle or at the end of the word. Together, sort the words into three lists: the /j/ sound at the beginning, the /j/ sound in the middle and the /j/ sound at the end of the word. Ask the children if they can see any patterns in the way the /j/ sound is spelt.

Write the words 'wag', 'rag' and 'hug' on the board. Read the words together and establish that the 'g' at the end is a hard /g/ sound. Ask: 'What happens if I add an "e" to the end of these words?' Agree that the hard /g/ becomes a soft /j/ sound and the vowel becomes a long vowel sound.

Write the following words on the board: 'strange', 'page', 'change', 'huge', 'passage', 'village'. Ask volunteers to read the words in 'robot talk'. 'Robot talk' each word again with the group, pointing to each grapheme in turn. Discuss the relevant spelling rules.

Pupil practice

Pupil Book pages 4–5

Get started

This task reinforces the correlation between the /j/ sound and the '–ge' spelling. Encourage the children to read the words out loud.

Answers

1. *page*	*[example]*
2. rage	[1 mark]
3. strange	[1 mark]
4. range	[1 mark]
5. cage	[1 mark]
6. large	[1 mark]
7. barge	[1 mark]

Try these

This activity provides practice in choosing the '–ge' spelling for the soft /j/ sound. After the activity, talk about which words have a long vowel sound and which end in an /idge/ sound.

Answers

1. *wage*	*[example]*
2. bulge	[1 mark]
3. change	[1 mark]
4. charge	[1 mark]
5. message	[1 mark]

Now try these

If the children are struggling, remind them that they are practising the /j/ sound so they should find any /j/ sounds in the sentence and then remember the rule they have been practising.

Answers

1. *My grandfather's age is 72.*	*[example]*
2. She lives in a small cottage by the sea.	[1 mark]
3. Ed likes to sing on the stage.	[1 mark]
4. The clown's shoes are huge.	[1 mark]
5. I like to drink orange juice.	[1 mark]

Support, embed & challenge

Support

Recap the /j/ sound with these children using the words 'jump', 'jug', 'magic', 'Roger', 'huge' and 'page'. 'Robot talk' these words and, together, write them out and locate the different spellings of the /j/ sound.

Work with these children as they carry out the activities on Unit 1 Resource 1: Sort it out. (**Answers** /j/ sound: 'j' spelling: John, jam, join, jump, joy, jog; '–ge' spelling: huge, large, stage, wage, change, sage, charge)

Embed

Ask these children to complete Unit 1 Resource 2: Lunge for the sponge. (**Answers** 1. change 2. huge 3. page 4. orange 5. stage 6. sponge; words ending in '–ge': wage, age, large, page)

Ask the children to search in their reading books for words ending '–ge' and share their findings with a partner.

Challenge

Challenge these children, working in a group to create two lists, each with ten words. List 1: words with the '–ge' spelling after the letter 'r' or the letter 'n'. List 2: words ending '–age' that end in an /idge/ sound.

Point out that most of the words covered in these exercises end in '–age'. Explain that there are very few words ending '–ige', '–oge', '–uge' and '–ege'. Ask the children to investigate the meaning of two or three of the following: 'oblige', 'stooge', 'scrooge', 'beige', 'siege', 'privilege', 'refuge', 'deluge'.

Homework / Additional activities

Spelling test

Ask the children to learn one of the following lists of words for a spelling test. Challenge them to write sentences for five of the words on their list.

Core words		Support words		Challenge words	
age	large	age	stage	rage	cabbage
cage	orange	cage	huge	page	refuge
rage	village	rage	image	stage	engage
page	damage	wage	cabbage	huge	storage
stage	cabbage	page	orange	charge	usage
huge	cottage			orange	voyage
charge	passage			village	lounge
change				damage	

Collins Connect: Unit 1

Ask the children to complete Unit 1 (see Teach → Year 2 → Spelling → Unit 1). Note: the Collins Connect activities could be used with Unit 1 or 2.

Unit 2: Words ending in –dge

Overview

English curriculum objectives

- The /j/ sound spelt as '–ge' and '–dge' at the end of words

Treasure House resources

- Spelling Skills Pupil Book 2, Unit 2, pages 6–7
- Collins Connect Treasure House Spelling Year 2, Unit 2
- Photocopiable Unit 2, Resource 1: Circle time, page 89

- Photocopiable Unit 2, Resource 2: Bage or badge? page 90

Additional resources

- Word cards: cotta, gara, stora, bagga, cabba, voya, sausa, mana, packa, messa, knowle, porri; plus nine '–ge' ending cards and nine '–dge' ending cards
- Word cards: wage, stage, huge, page, cage, nudge, splodge, smudge, hedge, sledge

Introduction

Teaching overview

The /j/ sound at the ending of a word is spelt '–dge' after a short vowel in short words (for example, 'bridge', 'pledge', 'dredge'), and in longer words where a short word with a short vowel is a root (for example, 'drawbridge', 'abridge'). 'Knowledge', 'porridge' and 'partridge' are the only longer words with this ending; most two- or three-syllable words ending in an /idge/ sound are spelt '–age'.

Introduce the concept

Recap on the work carried out in Unit 1: Write the words 'just', 'jam', 'wage' and 'change' on the board and ask a volunteer to explain how the /j/ sound has been spelt in these words. Challenge them to link the spelling to the position in the word. Together, remember some of the words covered in Unit 1,

for example, 'cottage', 'page', 'stage', 'huge', 'orange', 'change', 'charge'.

Write the following words on the board: 'bridge', 'fudge', 'midge', 'sledge'. Ask a volunteer to read them using 'robot talk'. Ask: 'How is the /j/ sound spelt here?' Explain that in short words ending /j/ with a short vowel sound, the /j/ sound is spelt '–dge'.

Write the words 'brige', 'fuge', 'mige' and 'slege' on the board. Ask a volunteer to read the words. Ask the children to write these words on their mini whiteboards, replacing the '–ge' ending with '–dge'. Talk about how adding 'd' to the ending changes the long vowel into a short vowel and gives us 'bridge', 'fudge', 'midge' and 'sledge'. Reverse the exercise using 'wadge', 'stadge', 'padge' and 'adge', changing the ending to '–ge' to create long vowel sounds for 'wage', 'stage', 'page' and 'age'.

Pupil practice

Pupil Book pages 6–7

Get started

This activity provides practice in spotting words ending '–dge'.

Answers

1. *splodge*	*[example]*
2. lodge	[1 mark]
3. nudge	[1 mark]
4. judge	[1 mark]
5. sledge	[1 mark]
6. fudge	[1 mark]
7. edge	[1 mark]

Try these

In this activity, the children write words ending '–dge' using picture clues.

Answers

1. *smudge*	*[example]*
2. fudge	[1 mark]
3. bridge	[1 mark]
4. fridge	[1 mark]

Now try these

The children spot the word that has been spelt incorrectly and rewrite the sentence, underlining the word they have corrected.

Answers

1. *My birthday <u>badge</u> has balloons on it.*	*[example]*
2. I lost my ball in the <u>hedge</u>.	[1 mark]
3. There is orange jelly in the <u>fridge</u>.	[1 mark]
4. Under the <u>bridge</u> lives a jolly old troll.	[1 mark]
5. The slimy slug is covered in <u>sludge</u>.	[1 mark]

Support, embed & challenge

Support

Create word cards for these words: 'wage', 'stage', 'huge', 'page', 'cage', 'nudge', 'splodge', 'smudge', 'hedge', 'sledge'. Cut the ending ('–ge' or '–dge') off each word and work with these children to recreate each word, trying each ending and reading the created words before deciding on which ending to use.

Provide these children with copies of Unit 2 Resource 1: Circle time. (**Answers** Words spelt '–ge': wage, stage, huge, cage, range; words spelt '–dge': bridge, fudge, judge, badge, sledge, edge, fridge. Long vowel: wage, stage, huge, cage, range; short vowel: bridge, fudge, judge, badge, sledge, edge, fridge. Pattern: words with a long vowel are more likely to end '–ge' than '–dge')

Embed

Ask these children to complete Unit 2 Resource 2: Bage or badge? (**Answers** 1. hedge 2. sledge 3. fudge 4. cabbage 5. package 6. fridge 7. huge 8. large)

Ask the children to work in groups. Give each group a set of word cards: 'cotta', 'gara', 'stora', 'bagga', 'cabba', 'voya', 'sausa', 'mana', 'packa', 'messa', 'knowle', 'porri'. Provide each group with a set of nine '–ge' ending cards and nine '–dge' ending cards. Ask them to add an ending to each word, explaining that they will have a few endings left over. Tell them to leave the words on their table then visit other tables to compare their answers.

Challenge

Ask these children to create a poster for the classroom explaining the different spellings for the /j/ sound.

Challenge them to create a list of (common/useful) two-syllable words that end '–idge', '–edge' and '–age'. After the activity, ask them to present their words and any discoveries they made. (Hopefully they will have discovered that most words ending in the /idge/ or /edge/ sound are spelt with '–age' at the end.)

Homework / Additional activities

Spelling test

Ask the children to learn one of the following lists of words for a spelling test. Challenge them to write a sentence for five of the words on their list.

Core words		Support words		Challenge words	
edge	sledge	edge	hedge	edge	fudge
bridge	fudge	bridge	nudge	bridge	porridge
lodge	pledge	lodge	badge	lodge	knowledge
fridge	wedge	fridge	sledge	fridge	budge
ridge	porridge	ridge	fudge	ridge	misjudge
hedge	knowledge			hedge	sludge
nudge	dislodge			badge	dislodge
badge				sledge	

Collins Connect: Unit 2

Ask the children to complete Unit 2 (see Teach → Year 2 → Spelling → Unit 2). Note: the Collins Connect activities could be used with Unit 1 or 2.

Unit 3: Spelling c before e, i and y

Overview

English curriculum objectives
- The /s/ sound spelt 'c' before 'e', 'i' and 'y'

Treasure House resources
- Spelling Skills Pupil Book 2, Unit 3, pages 8–9
- Collins Connect Treasure House Spelling Year 2, Unit 3

- Photocopiable Unit 3, Resource 1: Rice and mice, page 91
- Photocopiable Unit 3, Resource 2: Spelling spotter, page 92

Additional resources
- Word cards: city, circle, face, race, ice, mice, once, prince, police, sat, silly, list, pass, pasta, fussy, cats

Introduction

Teaching overview

The /s/ sound can be spelt 'c' before the letters 'y', 'i', and 'e'. The most common usage of this spelling pattern is at the ends of words with a long vowel sound, such as 'race' and 'rice', and in clusters such as '–ence' and '–ance', for example, 'pence' and 'chance'. In many of the contexts where it is used, it avoids the /z/ sound that a letter 's' would give ('rice' instead of 'rise'; 'icy' instead of 'busy'), although '–ence' and '–ense' endings sound the same. In other contexts, such as 'circle', 'cereal', 'cycle' and 'cell', the spelling needs to be learned.

Introduce the concept

Write the words 'mice', 'city' and 'lacy' on the board and ask the children to read the words.

Ask: 'What letter stands for the /s/ sound in these words?' Explain that sometimes we use the letter 'c' for the /s/ sound, particularly when followed by the letters 'e', 'i' and 'y' (but never 'o', 'u' or 'a'). Share more words with this spelling: 'rice', 'race', 'bicycle', 'cement', 'cell', 'pencil', 'mercy', 'spice', 'juice', 'fancy', 'cereal'. Circle the 'ce', 'ci' and 'cy' spelling in each instance.

Write the words 'rise' and 'rice' on the board and read them together. Explain that the /s/ sound is often spelt 'c' after a long vowel sound. Ask the children to work in pairs to think of three words that end with the sound /ace/ or /ice/. Share the ideas, writing them on the board, for example: 'ace', 'race', 'space', 'replace', 'disgrace', 'base', 'chase', 'case'; 'twice', 'rice', 'nice', 'price', 'ice', 'slice'. Point out that all of these words use the letter 'c' for /s/ except for 'base', 'chase' and 'case'.

Pupil practice

Pupil Book pages 8–9

Get started

This activity practises associating the letter 'c' with the /s/ sound and reinforces that it is spelt this way before 'e' 'i' and 'y'.

Answers
1. _city_ [example]
2. spice, nice [2 marks]
3. pencil [1 mark]
4. cell [1 mark]
5. cycle, recycle [2 marks]

Try these

This activity challenges children to remember how to spell words with 'ce' or 'ci'.

Answers
1. _circle_ [example]
2. slice [1 mark]
3. juice [1 mark]
4. face [1 mark]
5. cereal [1 mark]

Now try these

This activity practises spotting the spelling pattern in context.

Answers
1. _I celebrate my birthday once a year._ [example]
2. At the circus we saw some silly clowns. [1 mark]
3. We saw the cricket ball sail over the fence. [1 mark]
4. Your lacy dress is very fancy. [2 marks]
5. Lemons and limes are citrus fruits. [1 mark]

Support, embed & challenge

Support

Create a set of word cards for the following words: 'city', 'circle', 'face', 'race', 'ice', 'mice', 'once', 'prince', 'police', 'sat', 'silly', 'list', 'pass', 'pasta', 'fussy', 'cats'. Encourage the children to sound out each word in turn and decide if it has the /s/ sound in it. Agree that all the words have the /s/ sound. Then ask them to sort the words into those with the /s/ sound spelt 's' and those with the /s/ sound spelt 'c'. Help them to see the 'ce', 'ci' and 'cy' pattern, though use 'silly' to point out that, at the beginning of a word, 'si' is more common that 'ci'.

Ask these children to complete Unit 3 Resource 1: Rice and mice. (**Answers** The /s/ sound spelt 's': books, sat, list, sung, snip, swim; the /s/ sound spelt 'c': city, police, circle, pace, prince, mice, France, icy, cygnet, pencil, centre, rice. When the /s/ sound is spelt 's' it can be followed by any letter; when the /s/ sound is spelt 'c' it is often followed by 'i' or 'e'.) After they have completed the sheet, ask the children to point out the letter after the 's' or the 'c'. Help them to see

that the letter 'c' stands for an /s/ sound when it is followed by the letter 'y', 'i', or 'e'.

Embed

Ask these children to complete Unit 3 Resource 2: Spelling spotter to practise choosing the 'c' spelling when appropriate. (**Answers** fancy, centre, sing, dance, lace, peace, chase, juice, circle, mice, chance, voice, pencil, city, bicycle, bouncy)

Ask them to use the words in the Pupil Book, their spelling list below, the resource sheet, the Connect activity, the whole-class activities and any other spelling resources in the classroom to create a long list of words with the 'c' spelling for /s/.

Challenge

Ask these children to compare the spelling of 'rice', 'advice', 'ice', 'mice', 'icy', 'Nancy' and 'mercy' with the spelling of 'rise', 'busy', 'nosy', 'rosy', 'rise', 'noise', 'sunrise' and 'those'. Ask them to explain what sounds the 'c' and the 's' stand for in these words. (The 'c' stands for an /s/ sound while the 's' stands for a /z/ sound.)

Homework / Additional activities

Spelling test

Ask the children to learn one of the following lists of words for a spelling test. Challenge them to write a sentence for five of the words on their list.

Core words		Support words		Challenge words	
city	chance	city	mice	circle	France
circle	France	circle	once	city	once
face	once	face	prince	century	prince
race	prince	race	police	face	police
voice	police	ice	fancy	voice	bicycle
peace	bicycle			peace	fancy
ice	fancy			mice	mercy
mice				chance	

Collins Connect: Unit 3

Ask the children to complete Unit 3 (see Teach → Year 2 → Spelling → Unit 3).

Unit 4: Words beginning with kn– and gn–

Overview

English curriculum objectives

- The /n/ sound spelt 'kn–' and 'gn–' at the beginning of words

Treasure House resources

- Spelling Skills Pupil Book 2, Unit 4, pages 10–11
- Collins Connect Treasure House Spelling Year 2, Unit 4
- Photocopiable Unit 4, Resource 1: Four in a row, page 93

- Photocopiable Unit 4, Resource 2: Do you know which no? page 94

Additional resources

- Poster of words: gnome, gnaw, gnat, gnarled, know, knock, knee, knife, knit, knight, knot, kneel, knob, knives, knuckle, knelt, knack, knickers, knead, knocks, knave, kneecap
- Word cards: night, knight, new, knew, know, no, now, knot, not

Introduction

Teaching overview

There are a small number of words where the /n/ sound can be spelt 'kn–' and 'gn–'. This spelling reflects the Old English origins of the words where the initial consonant was voiced. There is no rule that can predict a 'kn–' or 'gn–': these words just need to be learned. However, the list is not extensive (particularly for words beginning 'gn–') with the key challenge for children being the difference between the homophones: 'know'/'no', 'knew'/'new', 'knight'/'night'.

Introduce the concept

Write the following sentence on the board: 'The knight knew the princess had knobbly knees'. Ask: 'How is the /n/ sound spelt in this sentence?' Agree that it is spelt 'kn–'. Write: 'The gnat bit the arm of the gnome sitting on the gnarled tree stump.' Ask: 'How is the /n/ sound spelt here?' Explain the meaning of 'gnarled' and 'gnat'. Explain that there are not many words with this spelling but they need to be learned.

Display a poster of these words: 'gnome', 'gnaw', 'gnat', 'gnarled', 'know', 'knock', 'knee', 'knife', 'knit', 'knight', 'knot', 'kneel', 'knob', 'knives', 'knuckle', 'knelt', 'knack', 'knickers', 'knead', 'knocks', 'knave', 'kneecap'. Continue to display the poster somewhere after the lesson.

Write the words 'night', 'knight', 'new', 'knew', 'know', 'no', 'now', 'knot' and 'not' on the board. Ask the children to turn to a partner and discuss the differences between the words. Ask them to make up a sentence for each. Share these as a class, for example: 'I looked up at the night sky.' 'The knight was tired after the battle.' 'Amir has a new pair of shoes.' 'Brendan knew he was right.' 'Do you know what time it is?' 'No, I don't.' Create word cards for these words. Hold the cards up at random and challenge the children to tell you the meaning.

Pupil practice

Pupil Book pages 10–11

Get started

This activity helps the children to become familiar with the 'gn–' and 'kn–' spellings.

Answers

1. *kneel*	*[example]*
2. knock	[1 mark]
3. gnaw	[1 mark]
4. gnash	[1 mark]
5. gnome	[1 mark]

Try these

This activity encourages the children to recall the words that they have learned with 'gn–' and 'kn–', while spotting some common homophones, easily confused words and common spelling mistakes.

Answers

1. *know, <u>gnow</u>, now*	*[example]*
2. <u>knaw</u>, gnaw, nor	[1 mark]
3. knot, <u>gnot</u>, not	[1 mark]
4. knew, <u>gnew</u>, new	[1 mark]
5. <u>knome</u>, gnome, home	[1 mark]

Now try these

This activity asks the children to find words that have been misspelt.

Answers

1. I _know_ the answer to the question. [example]

2. Samir's chest of drawers has blue knobs. [1 mark]

3. The brave knight had a sharp knife. [2 marks]

4. A gnat bit me on my knee. [2 marks]

5. There is a knot in Sam's knitting. [2 marks]

Support, embed & challenge

Support

Work with these children, focusing on the key homophone misspellings. Read the words on the flash cards from the introductory activity ('night', 'knight', 'new', 'knew', 'know', 'no', 'now', 'knot', 'not'). Read, sort and practise spelling the words together. Give pairs of children sets of the cards and ask them to test each other.

Ask the children to complete Unit 4 Resource 1: Four in a row. Afterwards, read all the words together.

Embed

Ask these children to complete Unit 4 Resource 2: Do you know which no? to further practise the common homophones with the 'kn–' spelling.

(**Answers** 1. know, 2. no, 3. know, 4. know, 5. new, 6. knew, 7. knew, 8. night, 9. knight)

Provide the children with the following clusters of words:

'knight', 'knee', 'knew'
'knot', 'know'
'now', 'not', 'new', 'no'

Ask them to make up a silly sentence using the words from each cluster. Tell them that they should recall their sentence next time they are trying to remember where to use the 'kn–' spelling.

Challenge

Challenge these children to write a short story using as many words beginning 'kn–' and 'gn–' as possible.

Homework / Additional activities

Spelling test

Ask the children to learn one of the following lists of words for a spelling test. Challenge them to write a sentence for five of the words on their list.

Core words		Support words		Challenge words	
gnome	knelt	gnome	knife	gnome	knight
gnaw	knife	gnat	knit	gnaw	knot
gnat	knives	know	knight	gnat	knead
gnarled	knit	knock	knot	gnarled	knuckles
know	knight	knee	knob	knock	knobbly
knew	knot			knelt	knave
knock	knob			knife	kneecap
knee				knives	knowledge

Collins Connect: Unit 4

Ask the children to complete Unit 4 (see Teach → Year 2 → Spelling → Unit 4).

Unit 5: Words beginning with wr–

Overview

English curriculum objectives
- The /r/ sound spelt 'wr–' at the beginning of words

Treasure House resources
- Spelling Skills Pupil Book 2, Unit 5, pages 12–13
- Collins Connect Treasure House Spelling Year 2, Unit 5
- Photocopiable Unit 5, Resource 1: Write and wrong, page 95

- Photocopiable Unit 5, Resource 2: Wriggles and wrinkles, page 96

Additional resources
- Word cards: write, wrong, wrap, wrist, wreck, wren, wriggle, wrinkle, wrestler, right, Richard, robin, robber, rat, round, when, what, wing, worm, wobble, will, went

Introduction

Teaching overview

There are about 20 words that primary-aged children might use that spell the /r/ sound 'wr–'. As with 'kn–' and 'gn–' spellings, these words need to be learned and there is no logical rule to help predict the spelling. Of these words, 'write' and 'wrong' are the two that lead to the most spelling mistakes, exacerbated by the homophones 'write'/'right'.

Introduce the concept

Give each table of children a set of words on separate cards: 'write', 'wrong', 'wrap', 'wrist', 'wreck', 'wren', 'wriggle', 'wrinkle', 'wrestler', 'right', 'Richard', 'robin', 'robber', 'rat', 'round', 'when', 'what', 'wing', 'worm', 'wobble', 'will', 'went'. Ask them to sort the cards into

two piles, deciding for themselves what criteria to use. Discuss the choices the children have used. Hopefully, some children will have chosen to organise the words by initial letter and others will have organised the words by initial sound. Ask all the groups to look at the words starting /r/ then to sort them into 'r' and 'wr' spellings.

Display a list of the most common words with this spelling: 'write', 'wrong', 'writing', 'wrote', 'wrap', 'wrist', 'wreck', 'wrapped', 'wren', 'wriggle', 'wreath', 'wrinkle', 'wring', 'wrapper', 'wrestler', 'wrack', 'wristband'.

Discuss the difference between the homophones: 'right'/'write', 'wrap'/'rap' and 'wrapper'/'rapper'.

Pupil practice

Pupil Book pages 12–13

Get started

This activity helps to embed the children's knowledge of the 'wr–' spelling pattern.

Answers

1. *writer*	*[example]*
2. wrote	[1 mark]
3. wrench	[1 mark]
4. wrap	[1 mark]
5. wreck	[1 mark]
6. wrinkle	[1 mark]
7. wriggle	[1 mark]

Try these

This activity provides practice in spotting key spelling mistakes mixed in with similar words.

Answers

1. *wrong, <u>rong</u>, wing*	*[example]*
2. rest, wrestle, <u>restle</u>	[1 mark]
3. <u>riggle</u>, wriggle, wiggle	[1 mark]
4. white, write, <u>riting</u>	[1 mark]
5. wren, <u>rinkle</u>, weak	[1 mark]

Now try these

This activity practises spotting key spelling mistakes within a sentence.

Answers

1. *When it is cold, you should <u>wrap</u> up well.*	*[example]*
2. My grandma's face is worn and <u>wrinkled</u>.	[1 mark]
3. Ana hurt her <u>wrist</u> when she fell.	[1 mark]
4. She ripped off the sweet <u>wrapper</u>.	[1 mark]
5. Sam <u>wrestled</u> his brother for the toy.	[1 mark]

Support, embed & challenge

Support

Return to the word cards with these children. Read each word in turn, emphasising the first sound. Sort the cards, first by initial sounds, then sort the /r/ words into 'r' and 'wr' spellings. Display all the words beginning 'wr–' and write the letters 'wr' on a mini whiteboard. Ask the children to give you a word beginning with these letters, referring to the words in front of them. Write each word in turn until all the words have been covered.

Recap on the difference between the meanings of 'right' and 'write'. Provide these children with copies of Unit 5 Resource 1: Write and wrong, which practises this. (**Answers** 1. wrong, 2. wrong, 3. right, 4. right, 5. Write, 6. wrong, 7. wrote, 8. write)

Embed

Ask these children to complete Unit 5 Resource 2: Wriggles and wrinkles.

(**Answers** correct words: wrong, wrinkle, wrote, wriggle, right, read, wrapped, wreck, wrapper, risked, write, wrap, wristband, wrist; incorrect words: ren, riggle, reck, rist, roat, rong, rinkle)

Provide the children with fresh copies of the resource sheet. Ask them to cut out the word cards and shuffle them. Tell them to work in pairs and race against their partner to see who is fastest at sorting all the words into correct and incorrect spellings. Tell them to check their partner's piles before declaring a winner.

Challenge

Ask these children to write a tongue twister using words beginning with the /r/ sound, including words with the 'wr' spelling.

Ask these children to find out the meaning of 'wrack', 'wreath' and 'wring'.

Homework / Additional activities

Spelling test

Ask the children to learn one of the following lists of words for a spelling test. Challenge them to write a sentence for five of the words on their list.

Core words		Support words		Challenge words	
wrong	wriggle	wrong	wrist	write	wren
write	wrinkle	write	wreck	wrong	wriggle
wrote	wring	writing	wrinkle	writing	wrinkle
wrap	wrapper	wrote	wrapper	wrote	wring
wrist	wrestler	wrap		wrap	wrapper
wreck	wristband			wrist	wrestler
wrapped				wreck	wristband
				wrapped	

Collins Connect: Unit 5

Ask the children to complete Unit 5 (see Teach → Year 2 → Spelling → Unit 5).

Unit 6: Words ending in –le

Overview

English curriculum objectives

- The /l/ sound spelt '–le' at the end of words

Treasure House resources

- Spelling Skills Pupil Book 2, Unit 6, pages 14–15
- Collins Connect Treasure House Spelling Year 2, Unit 6
- Photocopiable Unit 6, Resource 1: Apple on the table, page 97
- Photocopiable Unit 6, Resource 2: At the fair, page 98

Additional resources

- '–le', '–el', '–al' and '–il' word cards: wriggle, wrestle, knuckle, knobble, circle, table, apple, little, middle, jungle, cycle, people, bottle, horrible, level, label, angel, barrel, kennel, local, signal, metal, animal, hospital, magical, pencil, gerbil, until, tonsil, pupil

Introduction

Teaching overview

Many words end with an /ul/ sound. This ending can be spelt '-le', '-el', '-al' or '-il', but the '–le' spelling is by far the most common. The other spellings for this ending ('–el', '–al' and '–il') are covered in the next three units. Children should be encouraged to use '–le' for this ending sound when unsure of the spelling.

Introduce the concept

Provide groups of children with sets of '–le', '–el', '–al' and '–il' word cards. First, challenge them to find words with the 'wr–' or 'kn–' spellings for /r/ and /n/.

Next, tell them to read the words together in their groups and try to listen for a sound that is in each word. Agree it's the /ul/ ending. Explain that, although we often say these words with an indistinct vowel before the /l/, we spell this sound in different ways. It is likely that in the past more distinct pronunciation would have made the spelling more obvious.

Tell the groups of children to sort the words by their endings. Ask: 'Which pile of words is the largest?' Agree that it is the pile of words with the '–le' spelling. Explain that this is the most common of the endings and the one that you are going to practise first.

Pupil practice

Pupil Book pages 14–15

Get started

This activity encourages the children to locate the letters used in the /ul/ ending.

Answers

1. cab<u>le</u>	*[example]*
2. wobb<u>le</u>	[1 mark]
3. cast<u>le</u>	[1 mark]
4. simp<u>le</u>	[1 mark]
5. circ<u>le</u>	[1 mark]
6. feeb<u>le</u>	[1 mark]
7. rubb<u>le</u>	[1 mark]

Try these

This activity challenges the children to spell correctly words using phonics, knowing that the word will end in '–le'.

Answers

1. *ankle*	*[example]*
2. triangle	[1 mark]
3. table	[1 mark]
4. apple	[1 mark]
5. puzzle	[1 mark]

Now try these

This activity gives the children practice in correctly writing out words and using them in context.

Answers

1. *The old <u>castle</u> was in ruins.*	*[example]*
2. The pain in my foot makes me <u>hobble</u>.	[1 mark]
3. I have a <u>bobble</u> on top of my hat.	[2 marks]
4. My mum told me that I was in <u>trouble</u>.	[2 marks]
5. I love to eat a nice, juicy <u>apple</u>.	[2 marks]

Support, embed & challenge

Support

Read together some of the word cards with the '–le' ending from the opening activity. Model reading a word then breaking it down into individual sounds and write the letters or digraphs for these sounds.

Ask these children to complete Unit 6 Resource 1: Apple on the table. (**Answers** 2. p/ur/p/le, 3. a/pp/le, 4. t/a/b/le, 5. c/ir/c/le, 6. j/i/ng/le 7. p/i/m/p/le, 8. s/t/u/bb/le)

Embed

Ask these children to work in pairs. Challenge each pair to write six words that end '–le'. Have a race to see which pair can write six correct words the fastest.

Challenge the children to find and write down ten items from Unit 6 Resource 2: At the fair. There are 15 items: 'bottle', 'castle', 'toffee apple', 'people', 'battle', 'bicycle', 'table', 'circle', 'eagle', 'whistle', 'bubble', 'turtle', 'pineapple', 'juggle', 'triangle'.

Challenge

Challenge these children to think of words ending with '–le' that have a double consonant in them.

Homework / Additional activities

Spelling test

Ask the children to learn one of the following lists of words for a spelling test. Challenge them to write a sentence for five of the words on their list.

Core words		Support words		Challenge words	
circle	people	circle	cycle	circle	trouble
table	bottle	table	people	little	purple
apple	castle	apple	bottle	horrible	triangle
little	possible	little	horrible	jungle	double
middle	trouble	middle		cycle	available
horrible	purple	jungle		people	vegetable
jungle	triangle			castle	example
cycle				possible	

Collins Connect: Unit 6

Ask the children to complete Unit 6 (see Teach → Year 2 → Spelling → Unit 6).

Unit 7: Words ending in –el

Overview

English curriculum objectives
- The /l/ sound spelt '–el' at the end of words

Treasure House resources
- Spelling Skills Pupil Book 2, Unit 7, pages 16–17
- Collins Connect Treasure House Spelling Year 2, Unit 7
- Photocopiable Unit 7, Resource 1: Word match, page 99
- Photocopiable Unit 7, Resource 2: Choosing –le and –el, page 100

Additional resources
- '–le', '–el', '–al' and '–il' word cards: wriggle, wrestle, knuckle, knobble, circle, table, apple, little, middle, jungle, cycle, people, bottle, horrible, level, label, angel, barrel, kennel, local, signal, metal, animal, hospital, magical, pencil, gerbil, until, tonsil, pupil
- A poster with the key 25 words ending in '–el': model, parcel, tunnel, quarrel, hotel, travel, cancel, jewel, camel, flannel, squirrel, caramel, panel, towel, gravel, vowel, level, label, angel, barrel, kennel, shovel, sequel, funnel, tinsel

Introduction

Teaching overview
Although many words ending with the /ul/ sound are spelt with the '–el' ending, the list of words useful for primary school children is much smaller (about 25 words). Children should therefore be encouraged to learn the words with the '–el' ending, but to continue to use '–le' in situations where they are unsure of the ending.

Introduce the concept
Hand out the '–le', '–el', '–al' and '–il' word cards and ask the children to sort the cards into the different

spellings of the /ul/ sound. This time, once they've sorted the cards, tell them to discard all the cards apart from the words ending '–el'.

Display a poster with the key 25 words ending in '–el'. Ask a volunteer to choose a word from the poster and explain it to the rest of the class without using the word, for example: 'a small furry animal with a long fluffy tail that runs up trees'. The rest of the class must guess the word, using the poster for guidance.

Pupil practice

Pupil Book pages 16–17

Get started
This activity practises writing words ending in '–el', focusing on the ending.

Answers
1. squir<u>rel</u>   [example]
2. cara<u>mel</u>   [1 mark]
3. pan<u>el</u>   [1 mark]
4. tow<u>el</u>   [1 mark]
5. grav<u>el</u>   [1 mark]
6. vow<u>el</u>   [1 mark]
7. canc<u>el</u>   [1 mark]

Try these
In this activity, the children choose the spelling with the '–el' ending.

Answers
1. model   [example]
2. parcel   [1 mark]
3. tunnel   [1 mark]
4. quarrel   [1 mark]
5. hotel   [1 mark]

Now try these
In this activity, the children use words ending '–el' in context, copying them out to practise the correct spelling.

Answers
1. Riding a scooter is a fun way to <u>travel</u>.   [example]
2. Work hard or I will <u>cancel</u> play time.   [1 mark]
3. There is a <u>jewel</u> in the queen's crown.   [1 mark]
4. I saw a <u>camel</u> with two humps.   [1 mark]
5. Mum used a <u>flannel</u> to wipe my face.   [1 mark]

Support, embed & challenge

Support

Take the word cards from the starter activity and add more word cards, such as 'model', 'parcel', 'tunnel', 'travel'. Cut the words into the start of the word and the '–el' ending. Ask the children to recreate the words and read them together.

Provide these children with copies of Unit 7 Resource 1: Word match. Encourage the children to read each word out loud.

Embed

Ask these children to complete Unit 7 Resource 2: Choosing –le and –el. (**Answers** 1. parcel, 2. middle, 3. quarrel, 4. jungle, 5. travel, 6. cycle, 7. horrible, 8. hotel) This activity combines words from Unit 6 and Unit 7.

First, ask the children to read the words from the resource sheet. Then ask them to discuss with a partner whether they think they all end in the /ul/ sound or if some of them sound as if they end with an /el/ sound.

Challenge

Ask these children to write sentences for the following clusters of words:

> 'tunnel', 'squirrel', 'travel'
> 'parcel', 'hotel', 'towel'
> 'camel', 'angel', 'jewel'

Homework / Additional activities

Spelling test

Ask the children to learn one of the following lists of words for a spelling test. Challenge them to write a sentence for five of the words on their list.

Core words	Support words	Challenge words
parcel	parcel	parcel
tunnel	tunnel	tunnel
travel	travel	travel
jewel	jewel	jewel
camel	camel	camel
squirrel	squirrel	squirrel
towel	towel	towel
vowel	vowel	vowel
cancel	cancel	cancel
hotel	hotel	hotel
quarrel		quarrel
kennel		kennel
funnel		funnel
		model
		angel
		shovel

Collins Connect: Unit 7

Ask the children to complete Unit 7 (see Teach → Year 2 → Spelling → Unit 7).

Unit 8: Words ending in –al

Overview

English curriculum objectives
- The /l/ sound spelt '–al' at the end of words

Treasure House resources
- Spelling Skills Pupil Book 2, Unit 8, pages 18–19
- Collins Connect Treasure House Spelling Year 2, Unit 8
- Photocopiable Unit 8, Resource 1: Green crystal, page 101

- Photocopiable Unit 8, Resource 2: Spelling trios, page 102

Additional resources
- '–le', '–el', '–al' and '–il' word cards: wriggle, wrestle, knuckle, knobble, circle, table, apple, little, middle, jungle, cycle, people, bottle, horrible, level, label, angel, barrel, kennel, local, signal, metal, animal, hospital, magical, pencil, gerbil, until, tonsil, pupil

Introduction

Teaching overview
After the '–le' spelling, the '–al' spelling is the next most common spelling of the /ul/ sound. There are many words suitable for primary school writing spelt '–al', more of which are adjectives ('equal', 'final', 'local', 'normal', 'natural', 'general', 'central', 'magical', 'royal') than nouns ('crystal', 'animal', 'hospital').

Introduce the concept
Return to the '–le', '–el', '–al' and '–il' word cards and ask the children to locate all the words with the '–al'

ending. Read them together and decide what sound each word ends with. Share the children's thoughts.

Read out the following sentences and ask the children if they can identify the word ending in '–al' in each sentence.

> John and James made sure that they had equal amounts of sweets.
> Amir knocked his shin on the pedal of his bicycle.
> The bell was the signal for the end of the lesson.

Pupil practice

Pupil Book pages 18–19

Get started
This activity practises writing words ending in '–al'.

Answers
1. equal [example]
2. admiral [1 mark]
3. canal [1 mark]
4. plural [1 mark]
5. material [1 mark]

Try these
In this activity, the children are challenged to write a word ending in '–al' from a picture prompt.

Answers
1. animal [example]
2. spiral [1 mark]
3. petal [1 mark]
4. oval [1 mark]
5. pedal [1 mark]

Now try these
In this activity, the children place given words ending in '–al' into sentences.

Answers
1. Ariella's trumpet is made of metal. [example]
2. John Thomson is a very musical person. [1 mark]
3. We had a great time at the festival. [1 mark]
4. We visited Granny in the hospital. [1 mark]
5. The children went through the portal to a magical land. [2 marks]

Support, embed & challenge

Support

Ask these children to write the following words on a mini whiteboard: 'cereal', 'plural', 'musical', 'metal', 'loyal', 'final'. Ask them to circle the endings of the words.

Ask the children to complete Unit 8 Resource 1: Green crystal. (**Answers** ending '–le': purple, possible, jiggle, wobble, circle, cable, simple; ending '–el': towel, squirrel, vowel, panel, jewel, tunnel, camel; ending '–al': general, digital, animal, natural, hospital, total, canal, final, crystal, signal)

Embed

Ask these children to complete Unit 8 Resource 2: Spelling trios. (**Answers** ending '–le': purple, possible, jiggle, wobble, circle, cable, simple; ending '–el': towel, squirrel, vowel, panel, jewel, tunnel, camel; ending '–al': general, digital, animal, natural, hospital, total, canal, final, crystal, signal)

Challenge the children to write five words that end '–al' in 30 seconds.

Challenge

Ask these children to sort the words from their spelling list (see below) into nouns and adjectives. Explain that some of the words, such as 'final' and 'local', can be nouns *and* adjectives, so they should put these words in both lists.

Homework / Additional activities

Spelling test

Ask the children to learn one of the following lists of words for a spelling test. Challenge them to write a sentence for five of the words on their list.

Core words	Support words	Challenge words
equal	equal	equal
final	final	final
local	local	local
signal	signal	signal
metal	metal	metal
animal	animal	animal
hospital	hospital	hospital
magical	magical	magical
normal	normal	normal
actual	actual	actual
arrival		arrival
digital		digital
natural		royal
general		natural
		general
		several
		central
		crystal

Collins Connect: Unit 8

Ask the children to carry out Unit 8 (see Teach → Year 2 → Spelling → Unit 8).

Unit 9: Words ending in –il

Overview

English curriculum objectives
- Words ending '–il'

Treasure House resources
- Spelling Skills Pupil Book 2, Unit 9, pages 20–21
- Collins Connect Treasure House Spelling Year 2, Unit 9
- Photocopiable Unit 6, Resource 2: At the fair, page 98
- Photocopiable Unit 7, Resource 1: Word match, page 99
- Photocopiable Unit 9, Resource 1: Fossil, gerbil, basil, page 103
- Photocopiable Unit 9, Resource 2: Memory test, page 104

Additional resources
- '–le', '–el', '–al' and '–il' word cards: wriggle, wrestle, knuckle, knobble, circle, table, apple, little, middle, jungle, cycle, people, bottle, horrible, level, label, angel, barrel, kennel, local, signal, metal, animal, hospital, magical, pencil, gerbil, until, tonsil, pupil

Introduction

Teaching overview
There are about 18 useful words for primary school teachers that end in a consonant + 'il'. In many of these words the '–il' ending is clearer to hear than the '–le', '–el' and '–al' endings. However, the difference might not always be easy to hear.

Introduce the concept
Return to the '–le', '–el', '–al' and '–il' word cards one last time. Give each group four mini whiteboards. Tell them to label each board 'le', 'el', 'al' or 'il' and choose a scriber for each word ending. Read out each word in turn. Ask the groups to decide between them whether the ending is '–le', '–el', '–al' or '–il' and write the word on the appropriate whiteboard.

Pupil practice

Pupil Book pages 20–21

Get started
This activity practises writing words ending '–il'.

Answers
1. penc<u>il</u>   [example]
2. per<u>il</u>   [1 mark]
3. bas<u>il</u>   [1 mark]
4. stenc<u>il</u>   [1 mark]
5. counc<u>il</u>   [1 mark]
6. gerb<u>il</u>   [1 mark]
7. unt<u>il</u>   [1 mark]
8. tons<u>il</u>   [1 mark]

Try these
In this activity, the children find the word that ends in '–il' from each group.

Answers
1. *pupil*   [example]
2. tonsil   [1 mark]
3. evil   [1 mark]
4. fossil   [1 mark]
5. daffodil   [1 mark]

Now try these
In this activity, the children use words ending in '–il' in context.

Answers
1. *I have a pet <u>gerbil</u> called Nibbles.*   [example]
2. One day I would like to visit <u>Brazil</u>.   [1 mark]
3. I saw a dinosaur <u>fossil</u> at the museum.   [1 mark]
4. I used a <u>stencil</u> to draw a flower.   [1 mark]
5. I was not hungry <u>until</u> I smelled the chips.   [1 mark]

Support, embed & challenge

Support

With these children, focus on the handful of words that will be useful to them: 'pencil', 'nostril', 'gerbil', 'until', 'pupil', 'evil', 'devil', 'fossil'. Read and spell them together. As a group, write out the words with a line to separate each phoneme.

Ask the children to complete Unit 9 Resource 1: Fossil, gerbil, basil.

Embed

Ask these children to complete Unit 9 Resource 2: Memory test. (**Answers** gerbil, nostril, fossil, basil, pupil, pencil)

Afterwards, carry out the activity as a whole class. Divide the class into two groups. Time how long it takes for group 1 to remember all the words. See if group 2 can beat their time.

Challenge

Ask these children, in pairs, to discuss the meaning of the following words: 'peril', 'council', 'civil', 'basil', 'tonsil'.

Provide these children with cut-out images from Unit 6 Resource 2: At the fair and Unit 7 Resource 1: Word match, as well as Unit 9 Resource 1: Fossil, gerbil, basil. Ask them to create a word search of words ending with the /l/ sound, using the images as inspiration.

Homework / Additional activities

Spelling test

Ask the children to learn one of the following lists of words for a spelling test. Challenge them to write a sentence for five of the words on their list.

Core words	Support words	Challenge words
pencil	pencil	pencil
peril	nostril	peril
basil	gerbil	basil
stencil	until	stencil
council	pupil	council
gerbil	evil	gerbil
until	devil	until
tonsil	fossil	tonsil
pupil		pupil
evil		evil
fossil		fossil
daffodil		daffodil
Brazil		Brazil
		civil
		devil
		nostril

Collins Connect: Unit 9

Ask the children to complete Unit 9 (see Teach → Year 2 → Spelling → Unit 9).

Unit 10: Words ending in -y

Overview

English curriculum objectives

- The /igh/ sound spelt '–y' at the end of words

Treasure House resources

- Spelling Skills Pupil Book 2, Unit 10, pages 22–23

- Collins Connect Treasure House Spelling Year 2, Unit 10
- Photocopiable Unit 10 Resource 1: Lock and key, page 105
- Photocopiable Unit 10 Resource 2: Crossword, page 106

Introduction

Teaching overview

The children will be able to read these short words with the letter 'y' spelling /igh/ but will not always associate 'y' with /igh/ when they come to spell them. However, at this stage there are not many of these words that the children will be using.

Introduce the concept

Ask the children to give you some words with the /igh/ sound. Write the words on the board, creating lists of words with the same spelling for /igh/, for example: 'bite', 'line', 'nice', 'night', 'light', 'lie', 'flies', 'tries', 'my', 'shy', 'why', 'rhyme', 'July', 'cry', 'dry'. Create a long list, suggesting plenty yourself that end in /igh/ spelt '–y'.

Ask the children to write on their mini whiteboards all the words from the list that have the /igh/ sound at the end of the word. Ask the children to rub out all the words where /igh/ is spelt 'igh', then all the words with /igh/spelt 'ie'. Discuss the spelling of the words that are left.

Pupil practice

Pupil Book pages 22–23

Get started

This activity helps to associate 'y' as an alternative spelling for /igh/ in the children's minds.

Answers

–igh	–ie	–y
high [1 mark]	pie [1 mark]	fly [example]
sigh [1 mark]	tie [1 mark]	shy [1 mark]
		why [1 mark]

Try these

In this activity, the children reorder letters to make words, reminding themselves that this spelling for /igh/ is often found at the end of words.

Answers

1. *by*	[example]
2. my	[1 mark]
3. fry	[1 mark]
4. sky	[1 mark]

Now try these

This activity places 'y' for /igh/ words in context.

Answers

1. *When Joel woke up, the <u>sky</u> was blue.*	[example]
2. "Oh, please don't <u>cry</u>," said Raj.	[1 mark]
3. Morwenna is a <u>shy</u>, quiet girl.	[1 mark]
4. "<u>Why</u> are you late?" asked the teacher.	[1 mark]
5. I like to <u>fry</u> eggs in the morning.	[1 mark]

Support, embed & challenge

Support

Cut out the words from Unit 10 Resource 1: Lock and key and ask these children to sort them into the four ways of spelling the /igh/ sound: 'i' as in 'find', 'i_e' as in 'smile', 'ie' as in 'flies' and 'y' as in 'shy'.

Give each child a copy of Unit 10 Resource 1: Lock and key and ask them to complete the activity.

Embed

Ask these children to complete Unit 10 Resource 2: Crossword. (**Answers** Across: 1. rhyme, 3. deny, 6. fry, 7. July, 8. fly, 10. python; Down: 2. magnify, 4. cycle, 5. supply, 9. why)

At first, give the children the crossword with the words from the bottom folded back. Ask them to

attempt to complete it without these clues. After a few minutes, ask them to fold back the bottom of the page to help them finish.

After they have completed the activity, talk about the words 'cycle', 'rhyme' and 'python'. Ask: 'Where is the /igh/ sound here?' Talk about other words with this spelling: 'pylon', 'dynamic', 'byte'.

Challenge

Provide these children with the following list of words: 'rhyme', 'byte', 'cycle', 'dynamic', 'hyphen', 'pylon', 'python'. Ask them to make up a silly paragraph using these words to help them remember the shared spelling pattern.

Homework / Additional activities

Spelling test

Ask the children to learn one of the following lists of words for a spelling test. Challenge them to write a sentence for five of the words on their list.

Core words	Support words	Challenge words
by	by	why
my	my	sky
fry	fry	dry
cry	cry	shy
fly	fly	July
why	why	try
sky	sky	sty
dry	dry	deny
try	try	supply
July	July	rely
shy		magnify
deny		identify
supply		rhyme
rely		python
		cycle

Collins Connect: Unit 10

Ask the children to complete Unit 10 (see Teach → Year 2 → Spelling → Unit 10).

Review unit 1

A. Children look at the groups of words. They write the word with the spelling mistake in each group, then cross it out and write the correct spelling.

1. ~~brige~~ bridge   *[example]*

2. ~~sity~~ city   [1 mark]

3. ~~uncel~~ uncle   [1 mark]

4. ~~towle~~ towel   [1 mark]

5. ~~rong~~ wrong   [1 mark]

B. Children look at the pictures and write the words.

1. *pencil*   *[example]*

2. squirrel   [1 mark]

3. cereal   [1 mark]

4. pedal   [1 mark]

5. pupils   [1 mark]

C. Children look at the pairs of words and copy the word with the correct spelling in each pair.

1. *kneel*   *[example]*

2. gnome   [1 mark]

3. fancy   [1 mark]

4. simple   [1 mark]

5. sledge   [1 mark]

6. large   [1 mark]

D. Children find the spelling mistake in each sentence. They then rewrite the sentence with the correct spelling and underline the correct spelling.

1. *Snow White heard a <u>knock</u> at the door.*   *[example]*

2. Outside there was an old lady selling <u>lace</u>.   [1 mark]

3. There was something <u>wrong</u> with the old lady.   [1 mark]

4. Snow White invited the old lady into the <u>cottage</u>.   [1 mark]

5. The old lady gave Snow White a shiny <u>apple</u>.   [1 mark]

Unit 11: Adding –es to words ending in –y

Overview

English curriculum objectives
- Adding '–es' to nouns and verbs ending in '–y'

Treasure House resources
- Spelling Skills Pupil Book 2, Unit 11, pages 26–27
- Collins Connect Treasure House Spelling Year 2, Unit 11

- Photocopiable Unit 1, Resource 1: Sort it out, page 87
- Photocopiable Unit 10, Resource 1: Lock and key, page 105
- Photocopiable Unit 11, Resource 1: Rule spotter, page 107
- Photocopiable Unit 11, Resource 2: One welly, two wellies, page 108

Introduction

Teaching overview

When adding '–s' to words ending in '–y', we first need to turn the 'y' into an 'i', then add '–es' (rather than just '–s'). Or, if the children find it easier, remove the 'y' and add '–ies'. This spelling pattern is needed when creating plurals for nouns ending in '–y' ('bunny' → 'bunnies') and for creating third person verbs ('marry' → 'marries').

Introduce the concept

Recap on the words covered in the last session, asking the children to remember words ending with the /igh/ sound spelt 'y': 'fly', 'cry', 'dry', 'try', 'apply', 'magnify', 'fry' and so on. Explain the rule for adding '–es' using 'fly' → 'flies'. Then work together to create 'cries', 'dries', 'tries', 'applies', 'magnifies', 'fries' and so on.

Ask: 'Why do we need to add "–es" rather than just "–s" after we've changed the "y" to an "i"?' Try reading 'applis', 'fris' and so on. Agree that this spelling would give us a short /i/ and not the word we want.

Explain that we also use this rule for words ending in consonant + 'y' when the 'y' stands for an /ee/ sound. Ask them to work in pairs to add '–s' to 'lorry', 'poppy', 'nappy', 'family' and 'carry'.

Ask: 'What sort of words are these?' Help them to see that some are nouns ('poppy', 'nappy') and some are verbs ('fly', 'carry'). Create some sentences for each, explaining how they change: 'There is one red **poppy** in the garden.' 'There are lots of red **poppies** in the garden.' 'Jo fetched a **nappy** for the baby.' 'Jo fetched **nappies** for the **babies**.' 'The birds **fly** over the house.' 'The bird **flies** over the house.'

Pupil practice

Pupil Book pages 26–27

Get started

This activity provides initial practice in spotting the difference between '–y' and '–ies' endings.

Answers

–y		–ies	
bunny	[example]	bunnies	[example]
sty	[1 mark]	sties	[1 mark]
reply	[1 mark]	replies	[1 mark]
dry	[1 mark]	dries	[1 mark]
fly	[1 mark]	flies	[1 mark]
hurry	[1 mark]	hurries	[1 mark]

Try these

The children practise changing a '–y' ending to '–ies'.

Answers
1. *dollies*　　　　　　　　　　　　　*[example]*
2. stories　　　　　　　　　　　　　[1 mark]
3. babies　　　　　　　　　　　　　[1 mark]
4. countries　　　　　　　　　　　[1 mark]
5. copies　　　　　　　　　　　　　[1 mark]

Now try these

The children locate the word that needs to change in a sentence.

Answers
1. *Holly has two ponies called Apple and Patch.*

　　　　　　　　　　　　　　　　　[example]
2. In the end, Cinderella marries Prince Charming.

　　　　　　　　　　　　　　　　　[1 mark]
3. Amy likes counting her pennies.　　[1 mark]
4. In the autumn the trees are full of berries.　[1 mark]
5. The baby cries all day and all night.　[1 mark]

Support, embed & challenge

Support

Cut out the words from Unit 1 Resource 1: Sort it out and Unit 10 Resource 1: Lock and key (rejecting any words already end in an 's' and reject 'I', 'my', 'mine' and 'wild'). Recap on the rule for this unit and, together, sort the words into two sets: words where the ending needs to change, and words where the ending doesn't need to change. Using mini whiteboards, practise adding 's' to the words ending in 'y'.

Provide these children with copies of Unit 11 Resource 1: Rule spotter and ask them to complete the activity. (**Answers** 1. berry, lorry, hurry, hobby; 2. buggies, armies, marries, worries)

Embed

Once these children have practised the rule, they then need to practise spotting words and occasions when the rule applies in context. Ask the children to complete Unit 11 Resource 2: One welly, two wellies, which provides practice adding '–s' or '–es'.

(**Answers** 1. wellies, bags, armies, hobbies, sunrises, buggies, jeeps, diaries, stories, surprises, bicycles 2. marries, worries, empties, thinks, sings, supplies, carries)

Provide the children with the words from Unit 10 Resource 1: Lock and key (removing those already ending in 's'). Ask them to stick the words down the right side of a piece of paper and write the plural or third person singular verb next to it.

Challenge

Ask these children to make the nouns in the following sentences plural:

The family went to the beach.
I ate a cherry and a strawberry.
I saw a red lorry and a yellow lorry.
I tried to run but there was a buggy in my way.
My sister was given a pet bunny for her birthday.
The pirate, Red Jim, had one enemy.
There is a fairy that lives at the bottom of our garden.

Homework / Additional activities

Spelling test

Ask the children to learn one of the following lists of words for a spelling test. Challenge them to write a sentence for five of the words on their list.

Core words		Support words	Challenge words	
dry	fairy	dry	story	penny
dries	fairies	dries	stories	pennies
fly	worry	fly	berry	marry
flies	worries	flies	berries	marries
story	bunny	story	carry	supply
stories	bunnies	stories	carries	supplies
berry	penny	berry	hurry	empty
berries	pennies	berries	hurries	empties
carry		carry	fairy	family
carries		carries	fairies	families
hurry		hurry	worry	enemy
hurries		hurries	worries	enemies
			bunny	
			bunnies	

Collins Connect: Unit 11

Ask the children to carry out Unit 11 (see Teach → Year 2 → Spelling → Unit 11).

Unit 12: Adding –ed to words ending in –y

Overview

English curriculum objectives

- Adding '–ed', '–ing', '–er' and '–est' to a root word ending in '–y' with a consonant before it

Treasure House resources

- Spelling Skills Pupil Book 2, Unit 12, pages 28–29

- Collins Connect Treasure House Spelling Year 2, Unit 12
- Photocopiable Unit 12, Resource 1: Hurried word cards, page 109
- Photocopiable Unit 12, Resource 2: A hurried word search, page 110

Introduction

Teaching overview

Units 12, 13 and 14 cover adding '–ed', '–er', '–est' and '–ing' to words ending in '–y'. Once the children have mastered adding '–es' to words ending in '–y', adding '–ed', '–er' and '–est' should be straightforward.

Introduce the concept

Write examples of the verbs from Unit 11 on the board, such as 'hurry', 'marry', 'fry', 'dry' and 'carry'. Ask the children to help you to add '–es' to these words. Then explain that, when we add '–ed' to one of these words, the rule is very similar: we turn the 'y' into an 'i' and then add '–ed'. Explain that the new words created are past tense verbs, for example: 'I **hurried** home.' 'Jasmine **married** a prince.' 'Penny **fried** an egg.'

Ask: 'What sort of letter comes before the "y" in the original words?' Point out that it is a consonant and explain that this rule only applies to words with a consonant followed by a 'y' at the end of a word. Clarify that this 'y' can make an /igh/ or an /ee/ sound.

Write these words on the board: 'carry', 'tidy', 'say', 'marry', 'play', 'delay', 'run', 'smile', 'hurry', 'reply'. Ask the children to write down the words from the list that the rule 'remove the 'y' and add '–ed' applies to. Agree that these words are: 'carry', 'tidy', 'marry', 'hurry', 'reply'. Discuss why the other words don't fit the rule. (They either don't end in 'y' or have a vowel before the 'y'.) Tell the children to change the 'y' to an 'i' and add '–ed' to the words they have written. Read the words together.

Pupil practice

Pupil Book pages 28–29

Get started

This pairing activity helps the children to observe the changes in a word when '–ed' is added.

Answers

–y		–ied	
worry	[example]	worried	[example]
supply	[1 mark]	supplied	[1 mark]
try	[1 mark]	tried	[1 mark]
apply	[1 mark]	applied	[1 mark]
reply	[1 mark]	replied	[1 mark]
fry	[1 mark]	fried	[1 mark]

Try these

This activity provides straightforward practice in adding '–ed'.

Answers

1. *studied*		*[example]*
2. cried		[1 mark]
3. spied		[1 mark]
4. fancied		[1 mark]
5. carried		[1 mark]

Now try these

In this activity, the children spot the misspelt word and correct it in context.

Answers

1. *Nia was late so she <u>hurried</u> to school.*   *[example]*

2. I was <u>worried</u> about the spelling test.   [1 mark]

3. I didn't know the answers so I <u>copied</u> them.
[1 mark]

4. I <u>cried</u> when I watched the sad film.   [1 mark]

5. My granddad <u>married</u> my granny a long time ago.   [1 mark]

Support, embed & challenge

Support

Cut out a set of word cards from Unit 12 Resource 1: Hurried word cards. Work with these children to create the words 'carry', 'copy', 'worry', 'study', 'fancy', 'hurry' and 'fry'. Next, work on each word in turn to change the 'y' to an 'i' and add '–es' and '–ed'.

Provide these children with copies of Unit 12 Resource 1: Hurried word cards and ask them to make the words on the sheet.

Embed

Ask these children to do the word search on Unit 12 Resource 2: A hurried word search.

Challenge the children to remove the '–ed' from the words that they have found in the word search and recreate the original root word (for example, 'carry', 'empty').

Challenge

Ask these children to put this sentence into the past tense: 'The birds fly up to their nest.' Discuss what word they wrote for the past tense of 'fly'. Agree that it is 'flew' (not 'flied').

Ask these children to attempt to add '–er' to 'copy', 'worry', 'study', 'carry', 'tidy', 'magnify' and 'identify'. Share their attempts. Ask: 'What did you do with the letter "y"? What words have you created?'

Homework / Additional activities

Spelling test

Ask the children to learn one of the following lists of words for a spelling test. Challenge them to write a sentence for five of the words on their list.

Core words	Support words	Challenge words
tried	fried	copied
copied	dried	hurried
hurried	cried	worried
worried	tried	studied
studied	copied	carried
carried	hurried	married
married	worried	tidied
tidied	studied	replied
replied	carried	emptied
emptied		denied
		magnified
		identified

Collins Connect: Unit 12

Ask the children to complete Unit 12 (see Teach → Year 2 → Spelling → Unit 12).

Note: the Collins Connect activities could be used with Units 12–16.

Unit 13: Adding –er or –est to root words ending in –y

Overview

English curriculum objectives
- Adding '–ed', '–ing', '–er' and '–est' to a root word ending in '–y' with a consonant before it

Treasure House resources
- Spelling Skills Pupil Book 2, Unit 13, pages 30–31

- Collins Connect Treasure House Spelling Year 2, Unit 13
- Photocopiable Unit 13, Resource 1: Funnier word cards, page 111
- Photocopiable Unit 13, Resource 2: Silliest sentences, page 112

Introduction

Teaching overview

Once the children have mastered adding '–es' and '–ed' to words ending in '–y' (after a consonant) they should have no problem adding '–er' and '–est' to similar words. In the previous two units, the children have been working with nouns (Unit 11) and verbs (Units 11 and 12). The words in this unit are mainly adjectives, with some verbs being used to create nouns ('carry' → 'carrier').

Introduce the concept

Draw the following table on the board.

	+ es	+ ed	+ er
carry			
worry			
copy			

Ask volunteers to come out and fill in words for the '+ es' and '+ ed' columns. Next, ask the children if they can predict the spelling for the '+ er' column. Agree with correct suggestions and ask volunteers to complete the table on the board.

Ask the children to write the word 'empty' on their mini whiteboards followed by 'empty + es', '+ ed', '+ er' and, for a further challenge, '+ est'. Help them to see that the rules are very similar.

Pupil practice

Pupil Book pages 30–31

Get started

This activity helps children to become familiar with the '–ier' and '–iest' endings.

Answers

1. *happier*   [example]

2. sandier   [1 mark]

3. merriest   [1 mark]

4. messiest   [1 mark]

5. cosiest   [1 mark]

Try these

This activity provides the children with basic practice in adding '–er' and '–est' to words.

Answers

1.	pretty	*prettier [example]*	*prettiest [example]*
2.	ugly	uglier [1 mark]	ugliest [1 mark]
3.	lazy	lazier [1 mark]	laziest [1 mark]
4.	heavy [1 mark]	heavier [1 mark]	heaviest
5.	mighty [1 mark]	mightier	mightiest [1 mark]

Now try these

This activity provides practice in context, with the children choosing between using '–er' or '–est' to make the sentence work. Before they start, help them to understand that they will know from the context of the sentence which ending is required.

If they are not sure, they should say the sentence out loud using one ending and then the other.

Answers

1. *Princess Navi is the <u>prettiest</u> princess in the world.* [example]

2. My jokes are <u>funnier</u> than yours. [1 mark]

3. I want to be the <u>wealthiest</u> person in the world. [1 mark]

4. Kerem is <u>busier</u> than me. [1 mark]

5. Today's test is <u>easier</u> than yesterday's. [1 mark]

Support, embed & challenge

Support

Cut out the cards from Unit 13 Resource 1: Funnier word cards and use these to recap on the spelling rules. Together, make up some sentences orally for the words created.

Ask these children to complete Unit 13 Resource 2: Silliest sentences. (**Answers** 1. baggiest, 2. silliest, 3. tastiest, 4. creakiest, 5. rustiest, 6. sunniest)

Embed

Remind these children of previous work on noun phrases. Remind them that a noun phrase can be a noun plus an adjective and give these examples: 'shiny coin', 'yucky dinner' and 'muddy field'.

Help the children to turn the adjective in each noun phrase into a comparative adjective ('shinier coin', 'yuckier dinner', 'muddier field') and a superlative adjective ('shiniest coin', 'yuckiest dinner', 'muddiest field').

Challenge

Work with these children in a group. Provide them with some of the words used in the activities: 'copy', 'cries', 'fried', 'copier', 'happier', 'funniest'. Ask: 'What sort of words are these? Which is a noun? Which is a verb? Which is an adjective? What sort of adjective is it?'

Ask these children to create nouns from these verbs: 'carry', 'copy', 'worry', 'magnify'.

Homework / Additional activities

Spelling test

Ask the children to learn one of the following lists of words for a spelling test. Challenge them to write a sentence for five of the words on their list.

Core words	Support words	Challenge words
earlier	happy	earlier
earliest	happier	busier
easier	happiest	tinier
easiest	busy	angrier
happier	busier	baggier
happiest	busiest	easiest
busier	funny	wealthiest
busiest	funnier	heaviest
funnier	funniest	knobbliest
funniest		cheekiest
tinier		
tiniest		

Collins Connect: Unit 13

Ask the children to complete Unit 13 (see Teach → Year 2 → Spelling → Unit 13).

Note: the Collins Connect activities could be used with Units 12–16.

Unit 14: Adding –ing to root words ending in –y

Introduction

Teaching overview

Adding '–ing' to words ending in '–y' should be quite straightforward. However, children will remember that in some situations they need to turn the 'y' into an 'i', and this might cause some confusion.

Introduce the concept

Return to the verbs looked at in Unit 12: 'carry', 'copy', 'worry', 'study', 'fancy', 'hurry', 'fry' and 'try'.

Use these to recap on the rules for adding '–s', '–ed', '–er' and '–est'. Ask: 'What do you think happens when we add "–ing" to these words?' If turning the 'y' into an 'i' is suggested, model this and look together at 'carriing' and discuss whether we think it looks strange. Explain that, this time, the 'y' stays as it is and the suffix '–ing' is just added to the end of the word.

Pupil practice

Pupil Book pages 32–33

Get started

The children practise adding '–ing' without changing the root word.

Answers

1. *magnifying*	*[example]*
2. crying	[1 mark]
3. trying	[1 mark]
4. replying	[1 mark]
5. applying	[1 mark]

Try these

The children choose the correct spelling from each group of three.

Answers

1. *carrying*	*[example]*
2. frying	[1 mark]
3. spying	[1 mark]
4. supplying	[1 mark]
5. relying	[1 mark]

Now try these

The children locate the word in context that needs to have '–ing' added and then rewrite the sentence correctly.

Answers

1. *The monkey is <u>carrying</u> a basket.*	*[example]*
2. The pirates are <u>burying</u> their treasure.	[1 mark]
3. Calculators are useful for <u>multiplying</u> big numbers.	[1 mark]
4. I like to look at ants with my <u>magnifying</u> glass.	[1 mark]
5. I am <u>trying</u> very hard not to cry.	[1 mark]

Support, embed & challenge

Support

Write 'crispiest', 'dirtiest', 'boggiest', 'applying', 'tidying', 'hurrying', 'worrying' and 'copying' on the board. Read each in 'robot talk' and discuss the differences in spelling. Ask these children to help you return each word to its root word, then build them back up again.

Ask these children to complete Unit 14 Resource 1: Multiply endings. (**Answers** add '–ed': emptied, multiplied, simplified, dried, magnified, applied, copied, replied; add '–er': emptier, multiplier, simplifier, drier, magnifier, applier, copier, replier; add '–est': emptiest, driest; add '–ing': emptying, multiplying, simplifying, drying, magnifying, applying, copying, replying)

This provides practice for the four endings, '–ed', '–er', '–est' and '–ing', to help them remember when they do and do not need to change 'y' to 'i'.

Embed

Ask these children to complete Unit 14 Resource 2: Tons of sums. (**Answers** earliest, busiest, tiniest, boys, polishing, staying, angrier, burying, easier, wealthier, stories, emptiest)

This provides extra practice for each of the endings to familiarise children with determining whether or not to change the root word.

Challenge

Ask these children to put the following sentences into the past tense:

We are burying our time capsule in the garden.
Josh is bullying Sam at break time.
Finbar is tidying his room on Saturday.
Mum is applying cream to my sunburn.

Homework / Additional activities

Spelling test

Ask the children to learn one of the following lists of words for a spelling test. Challenge them to write a sentence for five of the words on their list.

Core words	Support words	Challenge words
frying	frying	frying
drying	drying	drying
crying	crying	crying
flying	flying	flying
copying	copying	copying
tidying	tidying	tidying
hurrying	hurrying	hurrying
carrying	carrying	carrying
worrying		worrying
replying		replying
		magnifying
		multiplying
		applying
		emptying
		partying
		envying
		bullying

Collins Connect: Unit 14

Ask the children to complete Unit 14 (see Teach → Year 2 → Spelling → Unit 14).

Note: the Collins Connect activities could be used with Units 12–16.

Unit 15: Adding new endings to root words ending in –e

Overview

English curriculum objectives
- Adding the endings '–ing', '–ed', '–er', '–est' and '–y' to words ending in '–e' with a consonant before it

Treasure House resources
- Spelling Skills Pupil Book 2, Unit 15, pages 34–35

- Collins Connect Treasure House Spelling Year 2, Unit 15
- Photocopiable Unit 15, Resource 1: Working hard, page 115
- Photocopiable Unit 15, Resource 2: Dance, dancer, dancing, page 116

Introduction

Teaching overview

When a word ends with an '–e', such as 'bake', 'raise', 'dance' and 'smile', the letter 'e' is removed before adding any suffix such as '–ing', '–ed', '–er', '–est' or '–y'. Although some of these suffixes start with the letter 'e', it is important that children still learn this rule as removing 'e' and adding the suffix (rather than just adding 'd', 'r' or 'st') both for their understanding of the word and for their grammar knowledge.

Introduce the concept

Write the words 'think' and 'bully' on the board. Ask: 'How do we add "–er" and "–ing" to these words?'

Agree the process, encouraging volunteers to explain the rule in each instance. Now write 'smile' on the board and ask the children to discuss with a partner how we might write 'smiled' and 'smiling'. Listen to the children's suggestions before explaining the rule.

Ask the children to write 'sleep', 'bake', 'cook', 'force', 'jump' and 'hate' as a list on their mini whiteboards. Tell them to rub out any words that the new rule doesn't apply to. Tell them to add '–ing' to the words that remain. (They should end up with: 'baking', 'forcing' and 'hating'.)

Pupil practice

Pupil Book pages 34–35

Get started

The children choose the correct spelling from two options.

Answers

1. *waving*	*[example]*
2. stony	[1 mark]
3. bravest	[1 mark]
4. trading	[1 mark]
5. exploding	[1 mark]

Try these

The children practise adding '–ing' and '–ed' to words ending '–e'.

Answers

1. *hiking, hiked*	*[example]*
2. blaming, blamed	[2 marks]
3. grazing, grazed	[2 marks]
4. saving, saved	[2 marks]
5. baking, baked	[2 marks]

Now try these

The children look for the wrong word in a sentence and then write the whole sentence correctly.

Answers

1. *When I hear a good joke, I can't help smiling.* *[example]*

2. The air gets very <u>smoky</u> when we light fires. [1 mark]

3. At last we <u>escaped</u> from the dragon. [1 mark]

4. Yesterday, we <u>danced</u> all afternoon. [1 mark]

5. My dog is always <u>chasing</u> rabbits. [1 mark]

Support, embed & challenge

Support

Provide these children with copies of Unit 15 Resource 1: Working hard. (**Answers** 1. baker, 2. tiler, 3. striker, 4. miner, 5. writer, 6. driver, 7. carer, 8. dancer)

This activity provides practice in removing '–e' and adding '–er'.

After the children have completed the resource sheet, encourage them to use the words on the page to write statements such as 'I like baking'.

Embed

Ask these children to complete Unit 15 Resource 2: Dance, dancer, dancing, which provides more practice adding the different endings.

(**Answers** 1. lacy, 2. bravest, 3. smiling, 4. whined, 5. behaved, 6. icy, 7. cutest, 8. rudest)

Provide the children with the following words: 'lace', 'slime', 'grime', 'noise', 'ice', 'juice' and 'stone'. Tell them to work with a partner to create an adjective for each word ('lacy', 'slimy', 'grimy', 'noisy', 'icy', 'juicy', 'stony').

Challenge

Give these children the following words: 'brave', 'noise', 'cycle', 'force' and 'cause'. Tell them to change each word, using a different prefix for each ('–ed', '–er', '–est', '–ing', '–y') and to then use the new word in a sentence.

Homework / Additional activities

Spelling test

Ask the children to learn one of the following lists of words for a spelling test. Challenge them to write a sentence for five of the words on their list.

Core words	Support words	Challenge words
user	user	user
using	using	used
used	used	saved
saved	saved	faced
faced	faced	taking
taking	taking	writing
writing	writing	chasing
chasing	chasing	dancer
dancer	dancer	dancing
dancing	closest	closest
closest		bravest
bravest		grimy
		juicy

Collins Connect: Unit 15

Ask the children to complete Unit 15 (see Teach → Year 2 → Spelling → Unit 15).

Note: the Collins Connect activities could be used with Units 12–16.

Unit 16: Adding new endings to one-syllable words with short vowel sounds

Overview

English curriculum objectives

- Adding '–ing', '–ed', '–er', '–est' and '–y' to words of one syllable ending in a single consonant letter after a single vowel letter

Treasure House resources

- Spelling Skills Pupil Book 2, Unit 16, pages 36–37
- Collins Connect Treasure House Spelling Year 2, Unit 16

- Photocopiable Unit 16, Resource 1: Double letters, page 117
- Photocopiable Unit 16, Resource 2: Running on a sunny day, page 118

Additional resources

- Word cards: nod, nodding, pat, patted, grin, grinning, sad, saddest, sun, sunny

Introduction

Teaching overview

When we add '–ing', '–ed', '–er', '–est' and '–y' to words that end with a short vowel followed by a single consonant (such as 'admit', 'run', 'bag', 'ship', 'slip' and 'tap') the final consonant is doubled before the suffix is added: 'chat' → 'chatted'.

Introduce the concept

Write the word 'slip' on the board. Ask: 'How do you think we add "–ing" to this word?' Demonstrate that if

we just add '–ing', the resulting word, 'sliping', would have a long /igh/ sound. Explain that we need to double the last consonant to protect the short vowel sound.

Write 'admit', 'run', 'slip', 'thin' and 'bag' on the board. Ask volunteers to come to the front and add '–ed', '–er', '–ing', '–est' and '–y' to the words (giving 'admitted', 'runner', 'slipping', 'thinnest' and 'baggy').

Pupil practice

Pupil Book pages 36–37

Get started

The children make the words by adding the ending to the short vowel words. They underline the double consonant.

Answers

1. _ru<u>nn</u>ing_   _[example]_
2. sla<u>mm</u>ed   [1 mark]
3. thi<u>nn</u>er   [1 mark]
4. fla<u>tt</u>est   [1 mark]
5. nu<u>tt</u>y   [1 mark]

Try these

This activity provides straightforward practice in following the rule.

Answers

1. _slimmer, slimmest_   _[example]_
2. thinner, thinnest   [2 marks]

3. fitter, fittest   [2 marks]
4. sadder, saddest   [2 marks]
5. fatter, fattest   [2 marks]

Now try these

The children look for the wrong word in a sentence and then write the whole sentence correctly.

Answers

1. _The woman is <u>petting</u> the cat._   _[example]_
2. My brother cried when he <u>popped</u> his balloon.   [1 mark]
3. Dad and I went <u>shopping</u> after school.   [1 mark]
4. We are having a picnic because it is a <u>sunny</u> day.   [1 mark]
5. The book was so <u>funny</u> that I laughed out loud.   [1 mark]

Support, embed & challenge

Support

Create word cards for these words: 'nod', 'nodding', 'pat', 'patted', 'grin', 'grinning', 'sad', 'saddest', 'sun', 'sunny'. Muddle up the words then ask the children to pair them up, sticking them down in two columns on a piece of paper. Tell the children to circle the last letter of each short word and the doubled consonant of each longer word.

Provide these children with copies of Unit 16 Resource 1: Double letters. (**Answers** 1. r/u/n, 2. r/u/nn/y, 3. d/i/g, 4. d/i/gg/er, 5. sh/o/p, 6. sh/o/pp/i/ng, 7. c/l/a/p, 8. c/l/a/pp/ed)

Embed

Write 'stop', 'tap', 'bike', 'trim', 'pack', 'wrap' and 'sing' on the board. Ask the children to tell you which of these words need to have the last letter doubled before adding '–ing'.

Ask these children to complete Unit 16 Resource 2: Running on a sunny day. (**Answers** 1. hopped [example], 2. chatting, 3. rubber, 4. sunny, 5. popper, 6. fittest, 7. batting, 8. dragged)

Challenge

Ask these children to create a poster for the class showing the rules for adding suffixes to words ending in '–y', '–e' or a single consonant.

Homework / Additional activities

Spelling test

Ask the children to learn one of the following lists of words for a spelling test. Challenge them to write a sentence for five of the words on their list.

Core words	Support words	Challenge words
sad	sad	sad
saddest	saddest	saddest
run	run	run
runny	runny	runny
pop	pop	pop
popped	popped	popped
shop	shop	shop
shopping	shopping	shopping
wrap		wrap
wrapper		wrapper
		admit
		admitted
		knit
		knitting

Collins Connect: Unit 16

Ask the children to complete Unit 16 (see Teach → Year 2 → Spelling → Unit 16).

Note: the Collins Connect activities could be used with Units 12–16.

Unit 17: Spelling words with al or all

Introduction

Teaching overview

The /or/ sound can be spelt 'a' before 'l' at the beginning or in the middle of words, or before 'll' at the end of short words, for example: 'ball', 'call', 'wall', 'fall', 'walk', 'stalk', 'also', 'always', 'alternative'. The children might find this easier to understand as /orl/ spelt 'al' or 'all'.

Introduce the concept

Write the words 'fork', 'ball', 'walk' and 'four' on the board. Read the words together then ask: 'What sound is in each word? How is it spelt?'

Organise the children into mixed ability groups. Challenge the groups to write down all the words they can think of where the /or/ sound is spelt 'a' before 'l' or 'll'. Share the words, giving one point for each correct word the groups have written down and a bonus point for each word that is unique to their group.

Pupil practice

Pupil Book pages 38–39

Get started

The children sort words with this spelling into two lists: 'al' and 'all'.

Answers

al		all	
stalk	[1 mark]	*ball*	*[example]*
talk	[1 mark]	fall	[1 mark]
		hall	[1 mark]
		stall	[1 mark]

Try these

The children add 'al' or 'all' to complete words with this spelling pattern.

Answers

1. *call*   *[example]*

2. bald   [1 mark]

3. also   [1 mark]

4. tall   [1 mark]

5. walk   [1 mark]

Now try these

The children use words with this spelling pattern in context.

Answers

1. *Giraffes are very <u>tall</u>.*   *[example]*

2. Mice are very <u>small</u>.   [1 mark]

3. I <u>always</u> do my homework on time.   [1 mark]

4. Humpty Dumpty fell off the <u>wall</u>.   [1 mark]

5. I love carrot and <u>walnut</u> cake.   [1 mark]

Support, embed & challenge

Support

Emphasise the relationship between the 'a' spelling and the /or/ sound by reading each of the words in these children's spelling test list using 'robot talk'.

Provide them with copies of Unit 17 Resource 1: Sort them all out. (**Answers** all, ball, talk, tall, fall, hall, small, walk, call, always)

Embed

Organise these children into pairs, and give each pair a mini whiteboard and pen. Set the timer for 30 seconds and challenge one child from each pair to write as many words as they can with this spelling. Their partner checks the words, turns over to the other side of the mini whiteboard and has 30 seconds to beat their score.

Organise the children into small groups. Give each child a mini whiteboard and have each group sit in a circle. Ask one child to write 'fall' on the whiteboard and pass it to the next person in the group who can change one letter to create a new word with the 'al'/'all' spelling. The children continue to change the word and pass the board on, for example, writing in turn: 'fall', 'ball', 'balk', 'walk', 'wall', 'mall', 'small', 'mall', 'tall' and so on. Words can be repeated.

Ask the children to complete Unit 17 Resource 2: Find them all. (**Answers** /orl/ spelt 'al': almost, always, almost, always, already, walk, talking, walk, walked; /orl/ spelt 'all': small, wall, called, small, all)

Challenge

Challenge these children, working in pairs, to write rhyming pairs of words with this spelling pattern. How many different rhyming endings can they come up with? ('ball'/'call', 'stalk'/'chalk', 'talking'/'walking', 'tallest'/'smallest', 'caller'/'smaller')

Homework / Additional activities

Spelling test

Ask the children to learn one of the following lists of words for a spelling test. Challenge them to write a sentence for five of the words on their list.

Core words	Support words	Challenge words
wall	all	wall
fall	ball	fall
hall	call	hall
small	tall	small
also	fall	also
walk	hall	walk
talk	small	talk
stalk	walk	stalk
always	talk	always
almost	always	almost
already		already
		altogether
		chalk
		stalk
		bald

Collins Connect: Unit 17

Ask the children to complete Unit 17 (see Teach → Year 2 → Spelling → Unit 17).

Unit 18: The /u/ sound spelt o

Overview

English curriculum objectives
- The /u/ sound spelt 'o'

Treasure House resources
- Spelling Skills Pupil Book 2, Unit 18, pages 40–41
- Collins Connect Treasure House Spelling Year 2, Unit 18
- Photocopiable Unit 18, Resource 1: Picture match, page 121
- Photocopiable Unit 18, Resource 2: Pairs, page 122

Additional resources
- Poster of words: above, another, brother, come, cover, done, dozen, glove, govern, honey, love, Monday, money, monkey, month, mother, none, one, other, oven, shovel, some, son, won, wonder, worry

Introduction

Teaching overview
The /u/ sound is spelt 'o' in several words (about 26): 'above', 'another', 'brother', 'come', 'cover', 'done', 'dozen', 'glove', 'govern', 'honey', 'love', 'Monday', 'money', 'monkey', 'month', 'mother', 'none', 'one', 'other', 'oven', 'shovel', 'some', 'son', 'won', 'wonder', 'worry'.

Introduce the concept
Write the letters 'e t m h r o' on the board and ask the children to help you reorder them to write the word 'mother'. When it comes to writing 'o', pause to discuss that it stands for the /u/ sound. Agree that 'muther' doesn't look at all right. Repeat the activity with 'e v l o' (love) and 'e c m o' (come).

Explain that there are quite a few words, most of which are fairly common, that spell the /u/ sound 'o'. Ask if anyone can suggest a word and write down any correct suggestions. Display a poster of the key words with this spelling. Read them together then display the poster in the classroom.

Pupil practice

Pupil Book pages 40–41

Get started
The children underline the /u/ sound, reinforcing the spelling pattern.

Answers
1. br<u>o</u>ther [example]
2. m<u>o</u>ther [1 mark]
3. n<u>o</u>thing [1 mark]
4. M<u>o</u>nday [1 mark]
5. w<u>o</u>rry [1 mark]
6. an<u>o</u>ther [1 mark]
7. gl<u>o</u>ve [1 mark]
8. m<u>o</u>nth [1 mark]

Try these
The children choose the correct spelling from three options.

Answers
1. *month* [example]
2. other [1 mark]
3. worry [1 mark]
4. nothing [1 mark]
5. brother [1 mark]

Now try these
The children locate the incorrectly spelt word.

Answers
1. *The <u>mother</u> cat has three kittens.* [example]
2. I threw a snowball at my <u>brother</u>. [1 mark]
3. I <u>worry</u> a lot about spelling tests. [1 mark]
4. <u>Nuthing</u> is tastier than chocolate cake. [1 mark]
5. Billy's mum is very proud of her <u>son</u>. [1 mark]

Support, embed & challenge

Support

Revisit this unit's 'Try these' activity (in the Pupil Book) and give the children more words to choose between: 'luv'/'love', 'wun'/'one', 'worry'/'wurry'.

Provide these children with copies of Unit 18 Resource 1: Picture match and Unit 18 Resource 2: Pairs. Tell them to cut out the word cards on Unit 18 Resource 2: Pairs. Ask them to find a word from the word cards for each picture on Unit 18 Resource 1: Picture match and to stick them in the spaces.

Embed

Ask these children to work in pairs and give each pair two copies of Unit 18 Resource 2: Pairs. Tell them to cut out the word cards and use them to play a game of pairs.

After the children have played the game a couple of times, tell them to use the word cards to test each other on the spellings of the words.

Challenge

Ask these children to talk about how to spell these words: 'son'/'sun', 'wonder'/'wander', 'funny'/'honey', 'love'/'stove', 'shovel'/'hovel', 'worry'/'hurry'.

Homework / Additional activities

Spelling test

Ask the children to learn one of the following lists of words for a spelling test. Challenge them to write a sentence for five of the words on their list.

Core words	Support words	Challenge words
one	one	none
none	none	done
come	come	other
some	some	mother
done	done	brother
other	other	Monday
mother	mother	love
brother	brother	above
Monday	Monday	another
love	love	cover
above		month
another		money
cover		honey
month		oven
money		

Collins Connect: Unit 18

Ask the children to complete Unit 18 (see Teach → Year 2 → Spelling → Unit 18).

Unit 19: The /ee/ sound spelt –ey

Introduction

Teaching overview

The /ee/ sound can be spelt '–ey' at the end of words, for example: 'chimney', 'turkey', 'monkey', 'donkey', 'alley', 'key', 'honey', 'money', 'journey', 'jersey', 'barley', 'chutney', 'curtsey', 'galley', 'jockey', 'kidney', 'medley', 'pulley'. When '–s' is added to these words, the root word stays the same: 'donkey' + '–s' = 'donkeys'. (The plural of 'money' is 'monies', but the use of this will not be common at Key Stage 1).

Introduce the concept

Ask the children if they can remember how to spell 'monkey', 'money' and 'honey'. Write the words on the board and recap on the /u/ sound spelt 'o'. Now

look together at the end of the words and point out the slightly unusual spelling of the /ee/ sound. Share the key words with this spelling and display these ('chimney', 'turkey', 'monkey', 'donkey', 'alley', 'key', 'honey', 'money', 'journey').

Discuss what might happen when we add '–s' to these words. Try out any options suggested (such as 'chimneies') and agree that it looks rather odd. Explain that we only need to add 's' to these words, giving us 'chimneys', 'turkeys', 'monkeys', 'donkeys' and so on. Point out that, as we can't count honey, we can't have a plural for it – only pots of honey, or lots of honey.

Pupil practice

Pupil Book pages 42–43

Get started

The children choose the correct spelling from three options.

Answers
1. *monkeys*   *[example]*
2. chutneys   [1 mark]
3. journeys   [1 mark]
4. trolleys   [1 mark]
5. valleys   [1 mark]

Try these

The children reorder letters to spell words ending in '–ey'.

Answers
1. *turkeys*   *[example]*
2. donkeys   [1 mark]

3. chimney   [1 mark]
4. pulleys   [1 mark]
5. keys   [1 mark]

Now try these

The children add '–s' to words ending '–ey' in context.

Answers
1. *There were three <u>donkeys</u> in the field.*   *[example]*
2. Smoke was coming out of all the <u>chimneys</u>.   [1 mark]
3. The city has lots of dark, twisting <u>alleys</u>.   [1 mark]
4. The gatekeeper carried a big bunch of <u>keys</u>.   [1 mark]
5. The <u>jockeys</u> are all trying to win the race.   [1 mark]

Support, embed & challenge

Support

Create word cards for the words in the support group's spelling list: 'journey', 'monkey', 'keys', 'money', 'honey', 'turkeys', 'valleys'. Cut up the words into phonemes and work together to recreate them.

Write the words 'cherry', 'chimney', 'kite', 'hat', 'monkey', 'bunny', 'donkey', 'thing', 'sofa' and 'lorry'. Ask these children to help you sort them into words where we just add '–s' to form the plural and words where we need to change the 'y' into an 'i' and add '–es'.

Ask the children to complete Unit 19 Resource 1: Finish it off. (**Answers** 1. turkeys, 2. curtseys, 3. trolleys, 4. alleys, 5. monkeys, 6. keys)

Embed

Ask these children to work in pairs to remember how we add '–s' to words ending in consonant + 'y' ('hurry' + '–s' = 'hurries'). Tell them to test each other in adding '–s' to 'pony', 'donkey', 'berry', 'monkey' and 'carry'.

Ask the children to complete Unit 19 Resource 2: Plural mix up, which provides a recap on the different ways plurals are formed and gives practice in spotting the different endings. (**Answers** 1. turkeys, 2. journeys, 3. curtseys, 4. trolleys, 5. jockeys, 6. alleys, 7. monkeys, 8. carries, keys, 9. hurries, chimneys)

Challenge

Ask these children to find out the meanings of these words: 'kidney', 'barley', 'galley', 'jockey'.

Homework / Additional activities

Spelling test

Ask the children to learn one of the following lists of words for a spelling test. Challenge them to write a sentence for five of the words on their list.

Core words	Support words	Challenge words
key	key	keys
keys	keys	money
turkey	turkey	honey
turkeys	turkeys	turkeys
valley	valley	valleys
valleys	valleys	journeys
journey	journey	chimneys
journeys	journeys	monkeys
chimney	monkey	donkeys
chimneys	monkeys	alleys
monkey	money	trolleys
monkeys	honey	curtseys
donkey		pulleys
donkeys		medleys
money		
honey		

Collins Connect: Unit 19

Ask the children to complete Unit 19 (see Teach → Year 2 → Spelling → Unit 19).

Unit 20: The /o/ sound spelt a after w and qu

Overview

English curriculum objectives
- The /o/ sound spelt 'a' after 'w' and 'qu'

Treasure House resources
- Spelling Skills Pupil Book 2, Unit 20, pages 44–45

- Collins Connect Treasure House Spelling Year 2, Unit 20
- Photocopiable Unit 20, Resource 1: Match the word, page 125
- Photocopiable Unit 20, Resource 2: Word duos, page 126

Introduction

Teaching overview

The next three units cover unusual vowel spellings after the /w/ sound. There are about 28 words with the short /o/ sound spelt 'a' after a /w/ sound that might be used in primary school. The list for Key Stage 1 is probably much shorter (about 14 words): 'want', 'was', 'what', 'wash', 'wasp', 'watch', 'wand', 'wander', 'wallet', 'swap', 'swan', 'squash', 'swamp', 'swallow'. (A more extensive list might include: 'wad', 'warrant', 'swat', 'qualify', 'quality', 'quarrel', 'quantity', 'quarry', 'squat', 'squalid', 'squabble', 'squalor', 'squander', 'squadron'.)

Introduce the concept

Write the letter 'a' on the board and ask the children what sound it stands for. Challenge them to think

of other sounds apart from the /a/ sound. Ask the children to write 'was', 'want' and 'what' on their mini whiteboards. Discuss the sound that the letter 'a' stands for in these words.

Write 'was', 'want', 'what', 'wash', 'wasp', 'watch', 'wand', 'wander' and 'wallet' on the board. Ask: 'What sound do these words have in common?' Say: 'The wasp wanted to wash' to help them to hear the /wo/ opening. Explain that the /o/ sound spelt 'a' only happens after a /w/ sound, which could be spelt 'w' or 'qu' and could be in the middle of the word. Display the following words and read them together, asking volunteers to circle the /wo/ cluster: 'want', 'was', 'what', 'wash', 'wasp', 'watch', 'wand', 'wander', 'wallet', 'swap', 'swan', 'squash', 'swamp', 'swallow'.

Pupil practice

Pupil Book pages 44–45

Get started
The children underline the letter that makes an /o/ sound in these words.

Answers

1. sw<u>a</u>n   [example]

2. squ<u>a</u>sh   [1 mark]

3. sw<u>a</u>mp   [1 mark]

4. qu<u>a</u>lity   [1 mark]

5. w<u>a</u>s   [1 mark]

Try these
The children write the word from picture clues.

Answers

1. wasp   [example]

2. wash   [1 mark]

3. swan   [1 mark]

4. watch   [1 mark]

Now try these
The children locate spelling mistakes in the sentences and correct them.

Answers

1. "I <u>want</u> a hamster!" said the boy.   [example]

2. Chen looked at his <u>watch</u> to see the time. [1 mark]

3. Please could I <u>swap</u> places with you?   [1 mark]

4. Don't forget to <u>wash</u> your hands.   [1 mark]

5. <u>Swallow</u> your food before you speak.   [1 mark]

Support, embed & challenge

Support

The most important words with this spelling are: 'want', 'was' and 'what'. Use a variety of simple sentences with these children: 'I want to go home.' 'I want my mummy.' 'I don't want to!' 'Matt wants a puppy.' 'Sita was walking.' 'Tim was running.' 'I was cooking.' 'What is that?' 'What happened?' 'What is the matter?' Read out the sentences in turn, mixing up the order. Ask the children to write down the word with the /wo/ sound that they hear in each sentence. If appropriate, display the words 'was', 'want' and 'what' during the activity.

Provide these children with copies of Unit 20 Resource 1: Match the word. (**Answers** 1. wasp, 2. swan, 3. wallet, 4. watch, 5. wand, 6. water, 7. squash, 8. swamp)

Embed

Return to the words in this unit's 'Get started' activity (in the Pupil Book). Ask these children to write the words as two lists: the /w/ sound spelt 'w' and the /w/ sound spelt 'qu'.

Ask the children to complete Unit 20 Resource 2: Word duos. (**Answers** 1. wasps, 2. wants, 3. swan, 4. squash, 5. swamp, 6. watch)

Challenge

Ask these children to write silly sentences using words with the /wo/ sound and then share them with the rest of the class. Challenge them to use at least three /wo/ words in each sentence. (Remind them that they can use 'watched', 'watching', 'swallows', 'wants', 'washes'.)

Homework / Additional activities

Spelling test

Ask the children to learn one of the following lists of words for a spelling test. Challenge them to write a sentence for five of the words on their list.

Core words	Support words	Challenge words
want	want	what
was	was	wash
what	what	wasp
wash	wash	watch
wasp	wasp	wander
watch	watch	wallet
wallet	swan	swap
swap	squash	swan
swan		squash
squash		swamp
swamp		squabble
		quarrel
		quality
		wand

Collins Connect: Unit 20

Ask the children to complete Unit 20 (see Teach → Year 2 → Spelling → Unit 20).

Unit 21: The /er/ sound spelt or after w

Overview

English curriculum objectives
- The /er/ sound spelt 'or' after 'w'

Treasure House resources
- Spelling Skills Pupil Book 2, Unit 21, pages 46–47
- Collins Connect Treasure House Spelling Year 2, Unit 21
- Photocopiable Unit 21, Resource 1: /er/ sound word search, page 127

- Photocopiable Unit 21, Resource 2: Choose the spelling, page 128

Additional resources
- Poster of words: work, word, world, worm, worse, worst
- Word cards: work, worm, word, world, worse and worst

Introduction

Teaching overview
This unit covers another unusual spelling following /w/. The /er/ sound can be spelt 'or' after 'w' in a handful of words. For Key Stage 1, there are only six key words: 'work', 'word', 'world', 'worm', 'worse' and 'worst'. Other words that are less common but worth learning are: 'worth', 'worthy' and 'worship'.

Introduce the concept
Explain to the children that the /w/ sound will be causing more problems. Write the word 'work' on the board. Ask: 'What sound do the letters "or" stand for here?' Agree that it is an /er/ sound. Explain that there are only a handful of words with this spelling but they need to be learned (especially 'work' and 'word'): 'work', 'word', 'world', 'worm', 'worse' and 'worst'. Display a poster of these words. Point out that these words can be used to make other words such as 'worldwide' and 'working'.

Pupil practice

Pupil Book pages 46–47

Get started
The children find the words with the /er/ sound from a range of words with an 'or' spelling.

Answers

work [example], worth, silkworm, worst, worm, world

[5 marks]

Try these
The children find the word from the box that the anagram makes.

Answers

1. *world*	*[example]*
2. working	[1 mark]
3. worthy	[1 mark]
4. worm	[1 mark]
5. workshop	[1 mark]

Now try these
The children spot the spelling mistakes in sentences.

Answers

1. *Birds think earthworms are a tasty treat.*   [example]
2. Churches, temples and mosques are places of worship.   [1 mark]
3. Workmen are digging up the road again.   [1 mark]
4. Today has been the worst day ever!   [1 mark]
5. I helped Granddad in his workshop today.   [1 mark]

Support, embed & challenge

Support

Focus on practising the key words 'work', 'worm', 'word', 'world', 'worse' and 'worst' with these children. Create a set of two word cards for each word and use the cards to play a game of pairs.

Provide these children with copies of Unit 21 Resource 1: /er/ sound word search and ask them to find the words in the word search, writing the words down as they find them.

Embed

Ask these children to complete Unit 21 Resource 2: Choose the spelling. (**Answers** 1. working, 2. Turn, 3. worst, 4. curly, 5. world, 6. word)

Ask the children to write down words with other spellings for the /er/ sound.

Challenge

Challenge these children to find as many words as they can with the root words 'work', 'word' and 'world' (for example, 'working', 'workshop', 'workforce', 'wordsmith', 'worldly', 'worldwide').

Ask these children to find out the meaning of 'worth', 'worthless' and 'worthy'.

Homework / Additional activities

Spelling test

Ask the children to learn one of the following lists of words for a spelling test. Challenge them to write a sentence for five of the words on their list.

Core words	Support words	Challenge words
work	work	work
word	word	word
world	worm	world
worm	world	worm
worse	worse	worse
worst	worst	worst
worth		worth
worthy		worthy
worship		worship
worldwide		worldwide
workshop		workshop
		worthless
		worldly

Collins Connect: Unit 21

Ask the children to complete Unit 21 (see Teach → Year 2 → Spelling → Unit 21).

Review unit 2

Pupil Book pages 48–49

A. Children look at the pictures and write the words.

1. *turkey*   [example]
2. bunnies   [1 mark]
3. wasp   [1 mark]
4. ball   [1 mark]
5. ponies   [1 mark]
6. monkey   [1 mark]

B. Children add the endings shown to the words. They write the new word. Remind them that they might need to change some letters.

1. *hurries*   [example]
2. babies   [1 mark]
3. copying   [1 mark]
4. flatter   [1 mark]
5. luckiest   [1 mark]
6. running   [1 mark]
7. joker   [1 mark]
8. coldest   [1 mark]

C. Children look at the pairs of words. They copy the word with the correct spelling in each pair.

1. *Monday*   [example]
2. sky   [1 mark]
3. brother   [1 mark]
4. squash   [1 mark]
5. alley   [1 mark]
6. watch   [1 mark]

D. Children find the spelling mistake in each sentence. They then rewrite the sentence with the correct spelling and underline the correct spelling.

1. *Pushkal dropped the glass he was <u>carrying</u>.*   [example]
2. My dress was the <u>fanciest</u> at the party.   [1 mark]
3. Only three boys <u>replied</u> to my invitation.   [1 mark]
4. Five <u>swans</u> swam past me.   [1 mark]
5. You must wear your <u>gloves</u> to play in the snow.   [1 mark]

65

Unit 22: The /or/ sound spelt ar after w

Overview

English curriculum objectives
- The /or/ sound spelt 'ar' after 'w'

Treasure House resources
- Spelling Skills Pupil Book 2, Unit 22, pages 50–51

- Collins Connect Treasure House Spelling Year 2, Unit 22
- Photocopiable Unit 22, Resource 1: Towards awards, page 129
- Photocopiable Unit 22, Resource 2: Meaning match, page 130

Introduction

Teaching overview

The key words with this spelling pattern for Key Stage 1 are: 'war', 'warm', 'towards', 'dwarf', 'award', 'reward', 'warn' ('warned', 'warning'). You might also want to cover: 'ward', 'warder', 'warden', 'wardrobe', 'warp', 'wart', 'swarm', 'swarthy', 'warmly', 'warmth', 'warthog'.

Introduce the concept

Recap on previous tricky spellings after the letter 'w', such as 'swan', 'watch', 'worm' and 'world'. Write 'Star Wars' on the board and wait for the children to read it. Underline the letters 'ar' in both words and ask what sound they represent. Agree that in 'Star' it is an /ar/ sound, and in 'Wars' it is an /or/ sound. Ask: 'Why is this? What dark force is at work here?' Agree that it is the letter 'w' causing problems again – in this case, making the letters 'ar' stand for /or/.

Pupil practice

Pupil Book pages 50–51

Get started

This activity provides practice spotting the 'war' spelling and associating that with the /wor/ sound.

Answers

warm [example], warp, swarm, ward, wart, war [5 marks]

Try these

In this activity, the children reorder letters to create words with the 'war' spelling. Remind them that all the words they are looking for will have the letter string 'war'. Encourage them to first write these letters down then see where the remaining letters might go, remembering they could be before or after 'war'.

Answers

1. *warble*	*[example]*
2. award	[1 mark]
3. dwarf	[1 mark]
4. wardrobe	[1 mark]
5. warmth	[1 mark]

Now try these

In this activity, the children find words that are spelt 'wor' when they should be spelt 'war'.

Answers

1. *The sky was blue and the sun was <u>warm</u>.*	*[example]*
2. Kamla <u>warned</u> us that the food was hot.	[1 mark]
3. I won an <u>award</u> for all my hard work.	[1 mark]
4. Dan's a wanted man: there's a <u>reward</u> for his arrest.	[1 mark]
5. The world should make peace, not <u>war</u>.	[1 mark]

Support, embed & challenge

Support

Focus on reading and copying the key words: 'war', 'warm', 'towards', 'dwarf', 'award', 'reward', 'warn'.

Ask these children to do the activity on Unit 22 Resource 1: Towards awards. (**Answers** 1. warm, 2. reward, 3. warning, 4. award, 5. towards, 6. dwarf)

Embed

Write the following pairs of words on the board: 'warm'/'alarm', 'war'/'bar', 'wart'/'start', 'warn'/'barn', 'award'/'yard', 'towards'/'cards'. Ask: 'Why don't these pairs of words rhyme?' Discuss the different pronunciations of the 'war' spelling.

Ask the children to do the activity on Unit 22 Resource 2: Meaning match. (**Answers** 1. award, 2. warm, 3. wart, 4. swarm, 5. war, 6. wardrobe, 7. warn)

Challenge

Ask these children to return to the words from Unit 20. Challenge them to create a list of non-rhyming pairs for these words, for example: 'what'/'bat', 'wash'/'bash', 'watch'/'batch', 'wander'/'gander', 'wallet'/'ballet', 'swap'/'map', 'swan'/'pan'.

Homework / Additional activities

Spelling test

Ask the children to learn one of the following lists of words for a spelling test. Challenge them to write a sentence for five of the words on their list.

Core words	Support words	Challenge words
war	war	war
warm	warm	warm
warmth	wart	warmth
towards	warn	towards
wardrobe	award	wardrobe
warm	towards	warm
wart	afterwards	wart
dwarf		dwarf
award		award
reward		reward
warn		warn
warning		warning
afterwards		afterwards
forward		forward
		awkward
		swarm

Collins Connect: Unit 22

Ask the children to complete Unit 22 (see Teach → Year 2 → Spelling → Unit 22).

Unit 23: The /zh/ sound spelt s

Overview

English curriculum objectives

- The /zh/ sound spelt 's'

Treasure House resources

- Spelling Skills Pupil Book 2, Unit 23, pages 52–53

- Collins Connect Treasure House Spelling Year 2, Unit 23
- Photocopiable Unit 23, Resource 1: A little bit of treasure, page 131
- Photocopiable Unit 23, Resource 2: A difficult decision, page 132

Introduction

Teaching overview

The words in this unit can be challenging for Year 2 children. The difference between the buzzing /zh/ sound in 'television' and the /sh/ sound in 'fish' is not very clear but a distinction should be made to avoid confusion later, particularly when comparing words ending '–sion' (which will often sound /zhon/) with those ending '–tion' (which sound /shon/). The buzzy /zh/ can be found in words ending '–sion' and words ending in '–sure' and children might find it easier to learn these endings concurrently.

Introduce the concept

Write the word 'television' on the board and read it together in 'robot talk'. Over-emphasise the /zh/ sound. Highlight its difference from the softer /sh/ sound in 'fish', 'shed' and 'station'. Explain that we find this sound in words that end '–sure' and '–sion'.

Write the following words on the board: 'television', 'decision', 'measure', 'leisure', 'treasure', 'erosion', 'explosion', 'pleasure', 'version', 'occasion', 'conclusion', 'confusion', 'collision'. Ask half the class to write the words ending in '–sure' on their mini whiteboards and the other half to write the words ending in '–sion'. Share the lists. Ask: 'Which list is longer?' Explain that '–sion' is a more common spelling pattern.

Tell the children that there is one more useful word that has this sound but is spelt differently: 'usual', which also has the /zh/ sound spelt 's'.

Pupil practice

Pupil Book pages 52–53

Get started

The children identify the 's' that stands for a buzzing sound in words.

Answers

1. televi_s_ion [example]
2. vi_s_ion [1 mark]
3. mea_s_ure [1 mark]
4. divi_s_ion [1 mark]
5. ero_s_ion [1 mark]
6. trea_s_ure [1 mark]
7. u_s_ual [1 mark]

Try these

In this activity, the children practise the difference between the /zh/ sound and the /sh/ sound.

Answers

/zh/ spelt s		/sh/ spelt sh	
decision [example]		fishing	[1 mark]
measure	[1 mark]	cushion	[1 mark]
usual	[1 mark]	mushroom	[1 mark]

Now try these

In this activity, the children spot misspelt words and correct them.

Answers

1. Feeding the ducks is a _pleasure_. [example]
2. The pirates are following a _treasure_ map. [1 mark]
3. I like to watch _television_ in the morning. [1 mark]
4. Suddenly there was an incredible _explosion_. [1 mark]
5. It was _unusual_ for Hassan to be late. [1 mark]

Support, embed & challenge

Support

The words in this unit will be difficult for many in Year 2. Concentrate on the five most useful or engaging words: 'usual', 'television', 'treasure', 'measure' and 'explosion'.

Provide these children with copies of Unit 23 Resource 1: A little bit of treasure and support them as they copy out the words. (**Answers** 1. explosion, 2. collision, 3. television, 4. treasure, 5. measure, 6. decision)

Continue to emphasise the link between the 's' and the /zh/ sound.

Embed

Ask these children to do the activity on Unit 23 Resource 2: A difficult decision. (**Answers** television, decision, measure, leisure, treasure, explosion, pleasure, version, occasion, conclusion, confusion, collision)

Ask the children to work with a partner and test each other to see who can remember the most words with this spelling.

Challenge

Ask these children to investigate words ending in '–ssion' (for example, 'discussion', 'impression' and 'passion') and decide how these words are pronounced (with a soft /sh/). Ask these children to share their findings with the rest of the class.

Homework / Additional activities

Spelling test

Ask the children to learn one of the following lists of words for a spelling test. Challenge them to write a sentence for five of the words on their list.

Core words	Support words	Challenge words
measure	measure	measure
leisure	treasure	leisure
treasure	pleasure	treasure
pleasure	television	pleasure
television	decision	television
decision	explosion	decision
explosion	confusion	explosion
conclusion		conclusion
confusion		confusion
collision		collision
		diversion
		version
		occasion
		erosion

Collins Connect: Unit 23

Ask the children to complete Unit 23 (see Teach → Year 2 → Spelling → Unit 23).

Unit 24: Adding the suffixes –ment, –ness, –ful, –less and –ly (1)

Overview

English curriculum objectives
- The suffixes '–ment', '–ness', '–ful', '–less' and '–ly'

Treasure House resources
- Spelling Skills Pupil Book 2, Unit 24, pages 54–55

- Collins Connect Treasure House Spelling Year 2, Unit 24
- Photocopiable Unit 24, Resource 1: Add it on! page 133
- Photocopiable Unit 24, Resource 2: Hopefully adding helpful suffixes, page 134

Introduction

Teaching overview

Learning to add these suffixes marks the beginning of a journey in manipulating and playing with language. When the children can turn verbs into nouns, adjectives into adverbs and nouns into adjectives, they can begin to write more complicated sentences. It starts here with adding simple suffixes to words where the root word doesn't need to change – in short, any root word that does not end in '–y'. The children need to avoid confusing the suffix '–ful' with the word 'full' and the '–ly' ending with an erroneous '–lly' ending.

Introduce the concept

Write the words 'treat', 'mad', 'hope', 'brave' and 'use' on one side of the board and the suffixes '–ful', '–ness', '–less', '–ment' and '–ly' on the other. Ask: 'What word do we get if we add these endings to any of the words?' Model adding different endings to different words, reading the words and deciding whether or not the new word exists.

Write the successful words on the board, for example: 'treatment', 'madness', 'hopeless', 'bravely' and 'useful'. Explain what a suffix is.

Explain that, when we add one of these suffixes to a word, as long as the word ends with any letter except 'y', we just add the suffix.

treat + ment → treatment

mad + ness → madness

hope + less → hopeless

brave + ly → bravely

use + ful → useful

Ask the children to add '–ly' to 'real', 'final', 'usual' and 'general'. Point out that these words all end in '–lly' because they have added '–ly' to a root word ending in '–l'. All other words will end in '–ly'.

Emphasise that the '–ful' suffix has only one 'l'. Remind the children to be careful not to confuse this suffix with the word 'full'.

Pupil practice

Pupil Book pages 54–55

Get started

The children practise adding suffixes.

1. *tiredness*	*[example]*
2. plainly	[1 mark]
3. entertainment	[1 mark]
4. playful	[1 mark]
5. heartless	[1 mark]

Try these

This activity provides practice in spotting that some words comprise root and suffix.

Answers

1. *sweetness – c) sweet*	*[example]*
2. fulfilment – d) fulfil	[1 mark]
3. thankless – a) thank	[1 mark]
4. shameful – b) shame	[1 mark]

Now try these

The children add the appropriate suffix to the underlined word in each sentence.

Answers

1. *Tortoises are known for their <u>slowness</u>.*	*[example]*
2. The kittens are <u>playful</u> little things.	[1 mark]
3. "This is stupid," said Thomas <u>crossly</u>.	[1 mark]
4. The duke is a cruel and <u>heartless</u> man.	[1 mark]

Support, embed & challenge

Support

Rather than practising adding suffixes to roots to create new words, work with these children on words they might want to spell with the suffix already added. Point out the different parts of each word. Together, spell: 'useful', 'careful', 'helpful', 'painful', 'harmful', 'likely', 'really', 'clearly' and 'quickly'.

Provide these children with copies of Unit 24 Resource 1: Add it on! (**Answers** really, likely, clearly, finally, quickly, useful, hopeful, painful, careful; really, lovely, finally, harmful, stressful, fearful)

Embed

Ask these children to write the words 'treat', 'mad', 'hope', 'brave' and 'use' on their mini whiteboards. Tell them to work in groups to decide whether the words are nouns, verbs or adjectives, pointing out that some words can be more than one ('treat' = noun and verb; 'mad' = adjective; 'hope' = noun and verb; 'brave' = adjective; 'use' = noun and verb). Now ask them to write 'treatment', 'madness', 'hopeless', 'bravely' and 'useful' on their boards. Ask: 'What sort

of words are these?' ('treatment' = noun; 'madness' = noun; 'hopeless' = adjective; 'useful' = adjective; 'bravely' = adverb)

Ask the children to work in pairs to investigate what happens to the word type before and after the suffix is added for: 'tired' + 'ness'; 'plain' + 'ly'; 'entertain' + 'ment'; 'play' + 'ful'; 'heart' + 'less'.

Ask the children to do Unit 24 Resource 2: Hopefully adding helpful suffixes to further practise adding suffixes. (**Answers** payment, movement, agreement, engagement, darkness, thickness, quickness, braveness, useful, powerful, careful, wonderful, thoughtless, worthless, timeless, fearless, usually, clearly, really, finally)

Challenge

Challenge these children to use two suffixes with the same root words, for example: 'help' + 'ful' + 'ness'. Ask them to experiment with 'help', 'use', 'forget', 'cheer', 'thought', 'point', '–ful', '–less' and '–ness'.

Ask these children to decide what sort of word (noun, verb, adverb or adjective) is created by each suffix.

Homework / Additional activities

Spelling test

Ask the children to learn one of the following lists of words for a spelling test. Challenge them to write a sentence for five of the words on their list.

Core words	Support words	Challenge words
really	really	really
quickly	likely	quickly
thickness	clearly	thickness
unfairness	finally	unfairness
useless	quickly	useless
hopeless	useful	hopeless
movement	helpful	movement
payment	painful	payment
useful	careful	useful
careful	hopeful	careful
		helpfulness
		usefulness
		forgetfulness
		cheerfulness

Collins Connect: Unit 24

Ask the children to complete Unit 24 (see Teach → Year 2 → Spelling → Unit 24).

Note: the Collins Connect activities could be used with Units 24 and 25.

Unit 25: Adding the suffixes –ment, –ness, –ful, –less and –ly (2)

Overview

English curriculum objectives
- The suffixes '–ment', '–ness', '–ful', '–less' and '–ly'

Treasure House resources
- Spelling Skills Pupil Book 2, Unit 25, pages 56–57

- Collins Connect Treasure House Spelling Year 2, Unit 25
- Photocopiable Unit 25, Resource 1: Lucky and luckily, page 135
- Photocopiable Unit 25, Resource 2: Heavily and angrily, page 136

Introduction

Teaching overview

Following on from their experience of adding '–es', '–ed', '–er' and '–est' to words ending in '–y' (Units 11, 12 and 13) the children should find the spelling here quite straightforward. When adding '–ment', '–ness', '–ful', '–less' and '–ly' to words with two syllables ending in a single consonant + '–y', the 'y' must first be changed into an 'i', for example: 'happy' + '–ness' = 'happiness'.

Introduce the concept

Recap on the learning from the last unit. Ask volunteers to suggest and then write on the board various words ending with the suffixes '–ment', '–ness', '–ful', '–less' and '–ly'.

Challenge the children now to write the words 'busy' + '–ness', 'penny' + '–less', 'merry' + '–ment', 'easy' + '–ly' and 'beauty' + '–ful'. Share the children's answers and agree the spelling rule: if the root word is two syllables long and ends in one consonant and '–y', we change the 'y' to 'i' and then add the suffix.

Now write 'shy', 'pay' and 'enjoy' on the board. Ask: 'How should we spell "shyly", "payment" and "enjoyment"?' Try changing the 'y' to an 'i' and agree that doesn't look right. Explain that short words that end in '–y' (such as 'dry', 'fly', and 'shy') and words that end 'vowel' + '–y' (such as 'pay', 'joy', 'play' and 'enjoy') retain their 'y', giving us 'dryness', 'shyly', 'dryly', 'joyful', 'playful' and 'enjoyment'.

Pupil practice

Pupil Book pages 56–57

Get started

This activity provides practice in identifying how many syllables a word has.

Answers

One syllable		Two syllables	
dry	[1 mark]	*angry*	*[example]*
sly	[1 mark]	happy	[1 mark]
		lucky	[1 mark]
		soppy	[1 mark]

Try these

In this activity, the children add suffixes to words ending in '–y', spotting when they do and do not need to change the 'y' to an 'i'.

Answers

1. *happiness*   *[example]*
2. soppiness   [1 mark]

3. slyly   [1 mark]
4. luckily   [1 mark]
5. angrily   [1 mark]
6. dryness   [1 mark]

Now try these

The children add '–ly' to words in context.

Answers

1. *The school band played <u>noisily</u>.*   *[example]*
2. <u>Brightly</u> coloured butterflies flew by.   [1 mark]
3. It was raining but <u>luckily</u> I had my umbrella.
                                          [1 mark]
4. Annabelle stretched and yawned <u>sleepily</u>. [1 mark]
5. <u>Amazingly</u>, no one was hurt in the accident.
                                          [1 mark]

Support, embed & challenge

Support

With these children, focus on the rules for spelling well-known words (rather than adding suffixes to create new words). Focus on words ending in '–ly' where the 'y' needs to change. Practise adding '–ly' to: 'easy', 'heavy', 'happy', 'angry', 'busy', 'lucky', 'noisy', 'speedy' and 'merry'.

Provide these children with copies of Unit 25 Resource 1: Lucky and luckily. (**Answers** lazily, prettily, nastily, noisily, unhappily, sleepily; easy + ly, happy + ly, dreamy + ly, naughty + ly, healthy + ly)

Embed

Ask these children to sort these words into those that need to change and those that don't: 'pay', 'lazy', 'enjoy', 'play', 'easy', 'shy', 'duty', 'sly', 'happy', 'silly'. Challenge them to add a suffix of their choosing to each, checking that the created word makes sense.

Ask the children to complete Unit 25 Resource 2: Heavily and angrily. (**Answers** easily, enjoyment, heavily, hastily, payment, angrily, merrily/merriment; greediness, joyless, loneliness, shyness, penniless, pitiless, gooeyness, nastiness)

Challenge

Provide these children with a long list of root words: 'brave', 'great', 'hard', 'sad', 'ill', 'end', 'use', 'home', 'agree', 'merry', 'duty', 'power', 'happy', 'usual', 'beauty', 'harm', 'care', 'good', 'treat', 'forget' and 'pain'. Encourage them to supplement their list with other words they have practised over the last two units. Challenge them to find the word that can take as many suffixes as possible (allowing them to add a 'y' or an additional suffix): 'worthiness', 'worthless', 'worthily', 'worthlessness', 'helpful', 'helpfulness', 'helpless' and so on.

Homework / Additional activities

Spelling test

Ask the children to learn one of the following lists of words for a spelling test. Challenge them to write a sentence for five of the words on their list.

Core words	Support words	Challenge words
easily	easily	easily
noisily	happily	noisily
business	luckily	business
loneliness	noisily	loneliness
penniless	unhappily	penniless
pitiless	lazily	pitiless
merriment	healthily	merriment
beautiful	beautiful	beautiful
plentiful		plentiful
enjoyment		enjoyment
		fanciful

Collins Connect: Unit 25

Ask the children to complete Unit 25 (see Teach → Year 2 → Spelling → Unit 25).

Note: the Collins Connect activities could be used with Units 24 and 25.

Unit 26: Apostrophes for contractions

Overview

English curriculum objectives
- Contractions

Treasure House resources
- Spelling Skills Pupil Book 2, Unit 26, pages 58–59
- Collins Connect Treasure House Spelling Year 2, Unit 26

- Photocopiable Unit 26, Resource 1: Contraction pairs, page 137
- Photocopiable Unit 26, Resource 2: Pull it together! page 138

Additional resources
- 'Don't' by Michael Rosen

Introduction

Teaching overview

Contractions in English are used for versions of the verb 'to be'. They can be in the present tense: 'I'm', 'you're', 'she's', 'he's', 'we're', 'they're'; the future: 'I'll', 'you'll', 'she's', 'they'll'; the conditional: 'I'd', 'she'd', 'we'd'; and as an auxiliary verb: 'I've', 'you've', 'they've', 'she's', 'I'd', 'you'd', 'she'd'. Contractions can combine verbs with 'not': 'don't', 'won't', 'can't' and so on. Contractions can be used with question words: 'who'd', 'how'll', 'when'll', 'why'd', 'what's'. In all cases, the apostrophe stands for a missing letter or letters.

Introduce the concept

Ask the children to role-play telling each other off. Listen to their ideas, pick out those with contractions and write them on the board, for example: 'Don't do that!' 'You'll fall!' 'I've told you once!' Circle the contractions and ask the children to tell you the long versions of the words. Write them underneath. Ask: 'What letters are missing from the short version?' Explain that the apostrophe shows that these letters are missing.

Write 'she is', 'they have' and 'why is' on the board. Work together to create the contraction, rubbing out the letters and replacing them with an apostrophe, then writing the remaining letters as one word.

Read 'Don't' by Michael Rosen.

Pupil practice

Pupil Book pages 58–59

Get started

The children match contractions to their longer form.

Answers

1. *I am – b) I'm*	*[example]*
2. could not – d) couldn't	[1 mark]
3. has not – a) hasn't	[1 mark]
4. she will – e) she'll	[1 mark]
5. there is – c) there's	[1 mark]

Try these

The children rewrite contractions as full words.

1. *he has got*	*[example]*
2. I will	[1 mark]
3. do not	[1 mark]
4. they have	[1 mark]
5. was not	[1 mark]

Now try these

The children replace selected words with contractions.

1. *"I'll take the dog for a walk," said Dad.*	*[example]*
2. "What's the problem?" asked Mum.	[1 mark]
3. "That's enough!" shouted Mrs Jones.	[1 mark]
4. "I'm not feeling very well," said Daisy.	[1 mark]
5. "Doesn't that work?" asked Riz.	[1 mark]

Support, embed & challenge

Support

For these children, focus on the most common contractions: 'don't', 'isn't', 'he's', 'we're', 'I'll', 'you're', 'they're', 'we'll', 'can't', 'didn't', 'hasn't', 'couldn't', 'it's'. Spend time writing out each word in short and long form, discussing the missing letter or letters in each instance.

Provide these children with copies of Unit 26 Resource 1: Contraction pairs. (**Answers** do not/ don't, is not/isn't, he is/he's, I will/I'll, you are/you're, cannot/can't, did not/didn't, it is/it's)

Ask them first to pair up the cards then to use the cards to play pairs.

Embed

Ask these children to complete Unit 26 Resource 2: Pull it together! (**Answers** don't, isn't, he's, I'll, you're, can't, when'll, where'll, didn't, it's, they're, we're, we'd, how's, that's, they've)

Challenge

Ask these children to work in a group to create a poster showing contractions starting with 'who' (such as 'who'll', 'who's', 'who'd'), 'what' (such as 'what's', 'what'll'), 'where' (such as 'where's', 'where'll'), 'when' (such as 'when's', 'when'll'), 'why' (such as 'why's', 'why've') and 'how' (such as 'how's', 'how're').

Homework / Additional activities

Spelling test

Ask the children to learn one of the following lists of words for a spelling test. Challenge them to write a sentence for five of the words on their list.

Core words	Support words	Challenge words
don't	don't	don't
isn't	isn't	isn't
he's	he's	he's
we're	we're	we're
I'll	I'll	I'll
you're	you're	you're
they're	they're	they're
can't	can't	can't
didn't	didn't	didn't
it's	it's	it's
who's		who's
where's		where's
		they've
		we'd

Collins Connect: Unit 26

Ask the children to complete Unit 26 (see Teach → Year 2 → Spelling → Unit 26).

Unit 27: Apostrophes to show possession

Overview

English curriculum objectives
- The possessive apostrophe (singular nouns)

Treasure House resources
- Spelling Skills Pupil Book 2, Unit 27, pages 60–61
- Collins Connect Treasure House Spelling Year 2, Unit 27

- Photocopiable Unit 27, Resource 1: Whose arm is this? page 139
- Photocopiable Unit 27, Resource 2: Wanted: missing apostrophe, page 140

Additional resources
- Small objects belonging to the children and a bag to put them in

Introduction

Teaching overview

The possessive apostrophe is probably the hardest spelling element for children to learn in Year 2, and it doesn't help that in everyday life they will see many misused apostrophes, which will only confuse them further. The possessive apostrophe in singular nouns is placed before the 's' and indicates possession and never a plural. To create even more confusion, children need to learn that the exception to the rule is the word 'its', which denotes possession without the apostrophe; 'it's' always means 'it is'.

Introduce the concept

Ask the children to pick up something that belongs to a neighbour (such as a pen or a rubber). Ask them to write down what they have on their mini whiteboards,

for example: 'Zak's ruler', 'Pushkal's jumper', 'Maisy's pen'. Share the phrases, writing them on the board and correcting them if necessary. Ask a volunteer to come to the front, circle one of the apostrophes and tell the class what its purpose is. Remind the children that you looked at apostrophes to show missing letters in the last unit; here, the apostrophe shows belonging. Encourage the children to look again at the phrase they wrote on their mini whiteboard and correct it if necessary.

Explain that we don't use an apostrophe when we talk about 'it'. Write these sentences on the board: 'Give the dog its bone.' 'Stroke its back.' 'Put on its lead.' Underline each instance of 'its'. Explain that 'it's' only ever means 'it is'.

Pupil practice

Pupil Book pages 60–61

Get started

This activity helps children to spot the apostrophe and focus on the difference between apostrophe + 's' for possession and 's' for plurals.

Answers
1. *Jorge's parents*   [example]
2. the chicken's eggs   [1 mark]
3. the children's homework   [1 mark]
4. the book's cover   [1 mark]
5. Meghan's bag   [1 mark]

Try these

In this activity, the children must work out which phrases describe possession – and therefore need an apostrophe – and which have plural nouns.

Phrases with apostrophe		Phrases without apostrophe	
Sandeep's bike	*[example]*	tables and chairs	[1 mark]
the car's wheels	[1 mark]	the horses in the field	[1 mark]
the sun's rays	[1 mark]	the new gym kits	[1 mark]

Now try these

In this activity, the children must work out which word in a sentence has an 's' for possession and is missing its apostrophe.

1. *The monkey's tail is very long.*   [example]
2. The rabbit's floppy ears are very soft.   [1 mark]
3. The coat's buttons are coming off.   [1 mark]
4. Those are Harita's shoes and gloves.   [1 mark]
5. Frank's socks are just like mine.   [1 mark]

Support, embed & challenge

Support

Focus with these children on correctly placing the apostrophe within a phrase. Ask each child in the group to give you a small object. Show the objects to the group and ask them to remember which item belongs to whom. Place them in a bag. Ask each child to remove an item from the bag and say what it is, for example: 'This is Chloe's hairband.' Ask everyone to write each sentence on their mini whiteboards.

Provide these children with copies of Unit 27 Resource 1: Whose arm is this? and ask them to complete the labels. (**Answers** Mabel's arm [example], Gracie's head, Charlie's leg, Stuti's hand, Niall's foot)

Embed

Ask these children to complete Unit 27 Resource 2: Wanted: missing apostrophe. (**Answers** 1. We rescued the wizard's wand from the cave. 2. Tashi and the two Janes found Bernie's necklace. 3. The chair's legs are wobbly. 4. The train's whistle is very loud. 5. It's too late to hear everyone's poems. 6. Take a large orange and take off its peel. 7. The computer's lights are flashing. 8. Look at that bird – I think its wing is broken.)

Write the following on the board: 'Todays spelling'; 'This years star pupil'; 'The months end'. Ask: 'Do we need an apostrophe in any of these?' Suggest reordering the sentences to find out: 'The spellings we are learning today'; 'The star pupil of the year'; 'The end of the month'; Tell the children: 'We can see that the "s" disappears when we reorder each of these sentences. That means it was only there to show possession, therefore we need an apostrophe.'

Challenge

Provide these children with a range of trickier sentences, some of which need two apostrophes: 'We found Toms note at our journeys end.' 'The cats bell was caught in its fur.' 'The weeks spellings fell behind Mrs Smiths desk.' 'The bottles lid fell off and its contents spilt everywhere.'

Homework / Additional activities

Spelling test

Ask the children to learn the following sentences, taking care to remember whether to use the word 'its' or 'it's':

It's raining

It's time to go.

Don't sit on that chair – its leg is wobbly.

Watch the milk – it's about to boil over.

Be careful with that book – it's precious.

Be careful with that book – its pages are falling out.

Don't pull its tail – it might bite.

Collins Connect: Unit 27

Ask the children to complete Unit 27 (see Teach → Year 2 → Spelling → Unit 27).

Unit 28: Words ending in –tion

Overview

English curriculum objectives
- Words ending in '–tion'

Treasure House resources
- Spelling Skills Pupil Book 2, Unit 28, pages 62–63
- Collins Connect Treasure House Spelling Year 2, Unit 28

- Photocopiable Unit 28, Resource 1: Action at the station, page 141
- Photocopiable Unit 28, Resource 2: Wrong direction, page 142

Additional resources
- A clean sock for each pair

Introduction

Teaching overview

Following on from the /zh/ sound spelt 's' in Unit 23, the children now need to learn the '–tion' ending that is pronounced /shon/. When the children are choosing between the '–sion' and '–tion' spellings, they should hopefully be able to hear the subtle difference in the pronunciation and choose '–sion' for /zhon/ (such as in 'decision') and '–tion' for /shon/ (such as in 'station'). Sadly, this rule is not foolproof as /shon/ can also be spelt '–ssion'. Children will find it useful to consider the two endings, '–tion' and '–sion', simultaneously. Although this spelling is a tricky one for Year 2, there are many useful words with this spelling, for example: 'action', 'station', 'direction', 'mention' and 'information'. 'Question' also has this spelling, though the ending has a harder sound.

Introduce the concept

Recap on the /zhon/ ending spelt '–sion' for words such as 'decision', 'television', 'explosion' and 'confusion'. Listen again to the /zhon/ ending. Now write the words 'action', 'station', 'direction' and 'mention' on the board. Ask the children to say the words very carefully. Ask: 'What sound cluster do you hear at the end?' Repeat each word, emphasising the softer /shon/ ending. Explain that they should listen carefully for the difference in sound when they are choosing between a '–sion' and a '–tion' ending.

Ask the children to sort these words into two lists, those spelt '–sion' and those spelt '–tion': 'information', 'decision', 'explosion', 'station', 'collection', 'action', 'collision', 'television'. They should work with a partner to read each word and write it in the correct list on their mini whiteboards.

Pupil practice

Pupil Book pages 62–63

Get started

In this activity, the children complete words by adding the '–tion' ending.

Answers

1. *education*		*[example]*
2. action		[1 mark]
3. collection		[1 mark]
4. portion		[1 mark]
5. section		[1 mark]
6. competition		[1 mark]
7. definition		[1 mark]

Try these

In this activity, the children choose the correct spelling out of three options.

Answers

1. *station*		*[example]*
2. section		[1 mark]
3. position		[1 mark]
4. question		[1 mark]
5. motion		[1 mark]

Now try these

The children choose the missing word from a number of options supplied.

Answers

1. *I love science <u>fiction</u> stories.*   *[example]*

2. My friend gave me <u>directions</u> to his house. [1 mark]

3. The factory chimneys filled the air with <u>pollution</u>. [1 mark]

4. I'm sure we can find a <u>solution</u> to the problem. [1 mark]

5. Meg chose the vegetarian <u>option</u>. [1 mark]

Support, embed & challenge

Support

Work with these children to practise spelling 'action' and 'motion' before moving on to the longer words. Spell them one syllable at a time.

Provide these children with copies of Unit 28 Resource 1: Action at the station. (**Answers** 1. motion, 2. potion, 3. action, 4. station, 5. question, 6. direction, 7. mention, 8. information)

Embed

Ask these children to complete Unit 28 Resource 2: Wrong direction. (**Answers** 1. station, 2. television,

3. information, 4. question, 5. decision, 6. pollution, 7. solution, 8. direction, 9. confusion)

After they have finished the activity, tell them to cut out the words from the box and place them in a cup or sock. Ask them to take the words out one at a time and test a partner on the spelling. They could compete to spell the most correctly.

Challenge

Ask these children to investigate words that spell the /shon/ ending '–ssion'. Encourage them to make lists of the words with the spellings '–tion', '–sion' and '–ssion'.

Homework / additional activities

Spelling test

Ask the children to learn one of the following lists of words for a spelling test. Challenge them to write a sentence for five of the words on their list.

Core words	Support words	Challenge words
motion	motion	motion
potion	potion	potion
action	action	action
station	station	station
question	question	question
direction	direction	direction
mention	mention	mention
information	information	information
situation		situation
connection		connection
solution		solution
		section
		pollution

Collins Connect: Unit 28

Ask the children to complete Unit 28 (see Teach → Year 2 → Spelling → Unit 28).

Unit 29: Homophones (1)

Overview

English curriculum objectives
- Homophones and near-homophones

Treasure House resources:
- Spelling Skills Pupil Book 2, Unit 29, pages 64–65

- Collins Connect Treasure House Spelling Year 2, Unit 29
- Photocopiable Unit 29, Resource 1: Write it right, page 143
- Photocopiable Unit 29, Resource 2: Here, hear! page 144

Introduction

Teaching overview

There are numerous homophones in English and they all need to be learned. This unit covers: 'right'/'write', 'sew'/'so', 'hear'/'here', 'there'/'their'/'they're' and 'whole'/'hole'. These need to be taught in context for the spelling patterns to have any meaning.

Introduce the concept

Write the words 'right'/'write', 'sew'/'so', 'hear'/'here', 'there'/'their'/'they're' and 'whole'/'hole' on the board. Go through the words with the children, discussing the meaning of each word. Have children work in pairs to construct sentences for each word.

Pupil practice

Pupil Book pages 64–65

Get started

The children pair up homophones.

Answers

1. *right – b) write*		*[example]*
2. sew – a) so		[1 mark]
3. hear – e) here		[1 mark]
4. there – c) their		[1 mark]
5. whole – d) hole		[1 mark]

Try these

The children choose the right homophone to fit the sentence.

Answers

1. *Please come <u>here</u>.*	*[example]*
2. They are putting on <u>their</u> shoes.	[1 mark]
3. I want the <u>whole</u> class to listen to me.	[1 mark]
4. That is the <u>right</u> answer.	[1 mark]

Now try these

The children choose a homophone from the box to complete the sentence.

Answers

1. *There's a <u>hole</u> in my bag.*	*[example]*
2. Can you <u>hear</u> the music?	[1 mark]
3. I am going to <u>write</u> a letter to my friend.	[1 mark]
4. I need to <u>sew</u> the hole in my trousers.	[1 mark]
5. <u>They're</u> staying at <u>their</u> granny's house.	[2 marks]

Support, embed & challenge

Support

With these children, focus on 'right'/'write', 'hear'/'here' and 'there'/'their'.

Provide these children with copies of Unit 29 Resource 1: Write it right and complete it as a group.

Embed

Have children work in pairs. Provide the pairs of children with the word cards from Unit 29 Resource 2: Here, hear! Ask them to cut out the words and place the words between them. Read one of the sentences from the homework list (or other sentences of your own creation) out loud and tell the children to race to pick up the correct card for the word you emphasise (omitting 'they're'). Find out who has the most cards at the end.

Organise the children into groups of three. One child makes up the sentences while the other two race for the cards. The children should swap roles at the end of each game.

Challenge

Challenge these children to come up with a sentence for each pair/group of homophones, for example: 'They're looking for their car over there.'

Homework / Additional activities

Spelling test

Ask the children to learn the following sentences:

There's a hole in my bucket.

Don't eat the whole cake.

Did you hear me calling you?

Come here now!

Write your name.

Turn right at the end.

Please can you sew on my badges?

It's so cold!

I've been here and there looking for you.

It's their turn to visit us.

They're coming home now.

Collins Connect: Unit 29

Ask the children to complete Unit 29 (see Teach → Year 2 → Spelling → Unit 29).

Note: the Collins Connect activities could be used with Units 29–31.

Unit 30: Homophones and near homophones

Overview

English curriculum objectives
- Homophones and near homophones

Treasure House resources
- Spelling Skills Pupil Book 2, Unit 30, pages 66–67
- Collins Connect Treasure House Spelling Year 2, Unit 30
- Photocopiable Unit 30, Resource 1: Pairs of pears, page 145

- Photocopiable Unit 30, Resource 2: Definition match, page 146

Additional resources
- Props for words: 'sea' (an image of the sea), 'blew' (a candle), 'pair' (a pair of socks), 'pear' (a pear), 'bare' (an image of bare feet), 'see' (some googly eyes or an image of eyes), 'blue' (something blue such as an item of clothing), 'bear' (a teddy bear).

Introduction

Teaching overview

This unit covers the homophones 'bare' (naked), 'bear' (an animal), 'bear' (to stand), 'pair' (two matching items), 'pear' (a fruit), 'blue' (a colour), 'blew' (the past tense of 'blow'), 'see' (look), 'sea' (ocean) and the near homophones 'quiet' (little noise) and 'quite' (rather). More able pupils are encouraged to investigate 'pare' (to peel or whittle) and 'bare' (to show or uncover).

Introduce the concept

Write these words on the board: 'bare', 'sea', 'pair', 'pear', 'blue', 'quiet', 'blew', 'bear', 'see', 'quite'. Ask volunteers to choose two words that sound the same – or very similar – and write them as a pair. After each pairing, ask the children what the different words mean. Display the props and ask them to choose one for each word.

Ask the children to work in pairs to think of silly ways to remember each spelling, for example: 'a bear has fluffy ears', saying the word 'blew' with a whistle at the end and so on.

Pupil practice

Pupil Book pages 66–67

Get started

The children match up words that sound the same or nearly the same.

Answers

1. *bear – b) bare*	*[example]*
2. pear – c) pair	[1 mark]
3. blew – e) blue	[1 mark]
4. sea – d) see	[1 mark]
5. quite – a) quiet	[1 mark]

Try these

The children choose the word to complete the sentence from two spellings.

Answers

1. *I have a cuddly teddy <u>bear</u>.*	*[example]*
2. The juicy <u>pear</u> was delicious.	[1 mark]

3. The <u>sea</u> is blue today.	[1 mark]
4. It is <u>quiet</u> in the library.	[1 mark]
5. I am <u>quite</u> good at playing the piano.	[1 mark]

Now try these

The children choose the word to complete the sentence from a list of ten words.

Answers

1. *I have a new <u>pair</u> of shoes.*	*[example]*
2. Can you <u>see</u> the bus coming?	[1 mark]
3. I <u>blew</u> out the candles on my birthday cake.	[1 mark]
4. I am <u>quite</u> sure that I am right.	[1 mark]
5. He walked on the sand with <u>bare</u> feet.	[1 mark]

Support, embed & challenge

Support

Use the word cards from Unit 30 Resource 1: Pairs of pears and the word props to recap on the spellings of the words covered in this unit. Use the cards to play a game of pairs.

Ask these children to work in pairs to create a short sketch for one of the words. As the children present the sketch, the other children must guess the word and say the spelling, using one of the word cards if they like.

Embed

Write the words 'bear' and 'bare' on the board and ask the children to tell you their meanings. Share a third meaning for 'bear', meaning to carry or take the weight of something, for example, 'I can't bear it!' or 'I'm not sure that chair can bear the weight of both of you'. Ask the children to write a sentence for each of the two meanings of 'bear'.

Ask the children to complete Unit 30 Resource 2: Definition match. (**Answers** blew – the past tense of 'blow', pair – two items that match or fit together, pear – a type of fruit that grows on a tree, bare – to be naked or uncovered, see – to look or to spot something, blue – the colour of the sky on a sunny day, sea – the ocean, bear – a large furry animal)

Challenge

Ask these children to practise using the following meanings by writing sentences:

'bare' (verb) to expose, for example: 'to bare one's teeth'

'pare' (verb) to peel or to carve away at something, for example: 'I pared down the number of people coming to the party'; 'I pared the apple'

Ask the children to present their findings to the rest of the class.

Homework / Additional activities

Spelling test

Ask the children to learn the following sentences:

The polar bear sleeps all winter.

We ran into the garden with bare feet.

There is a pear tree in the garden.

I cannot find a clean pair of socks.

The blue whale is the biggest animal in the sea.

I can see a rainbow in the sky.

Please be quiet, I'm reading.

We live quite a long way from the shops.

Collins Connect: Unit 30

Ask the children to complete Unit 30 (see Teach → Year 2 → Spelling → Unit 30).

Note: the Collins Connect activities could be used with Units 29–31.

# Unit 31: Homophones (2)

Overview

English curriculum objectives
- Homophones and near-homophones

Treasure House resources
- Spelling Skills Pupil Book 2, Unit 31, pages 68–69

- Collins Connect Treasure House Spelling Year 2, Unit 31
- Photocopiable Unit 31, Resource 1: Too many twos to remember! page 147 (including large versions)
- Photocopiable Unit 31, Resource 2: Definition mission, page 148

Introduction

Teaching overview
This unit covers the following homophones: 'one' (1), 'won' (the past tense of 'win'), 'to' (towards), 'two' (2), 'too' (also), 'be' (verb), 'bee' (insect), 'knight' (a soldier), 'night' (the opposite of 'day'). The trickiest of these is the word 'too', which continues to be misspelt by many throughout primary school and beyond.

Introduce the concept
Write 'be', 'knight', 'one', 'to', 'two', 'bee', 'night', 'won', 'too' on the board. Ask volunteers to choose two words that sound the same and write them as a pair. After each pairing, ask the children what the different words mean. After the words have been paired, look at the remaining word ('to', 'two' or 'too'). Ask a volunteer to add it to the correct pair. Provide a large version of the word cards on Unit 31 Resource 1: Too many twos to remember! and ask them to choose one to stick by each word on the board.

Ask the children to work in pairs to think of silly ways to remember each spelling, for example: 'the beeeeee buuzzzzzed'; 'the kind knight'; 'two owls go two-it two-oo'; 'I want to come tooooooo'.

Pupil practice

Pupil Book pages 68–69

Get started
The children match up words that sound the same.

Answers
1. *night – e) knight* [example]
2. be – d) bee [1 mark]
3. one – a) won [1 mark]
4. to – b) two [1 mark]
5. deer – c) dear [1 mark]
Numbers: one, two [2 marks]

Try these
The children choose a word to complete the sentence from a choice of two spellings.

Answers
1. *It is good to be kind to others.* [example]
2. The bee buzzed near my nose. [1 mark]

3. Mum says I eat too many sweets. [1 mark]
4. The moon shines at night. [1 mark]
5. It is time for us to go to bed. [1 mark]

Now try these
The children choose the word to complete the sentence from a list of nine words.

Answers
1. *I have two cakes. Would you like one?* [example]
2. I was happy when my team won the cup. [1 mark]
3. The knight put on his armour. [1 mark]
4. I went to the park. Jane came too. [1 mark]
5. I have two sisters and a brother. [1 mark]

Support, embed & challenge

Support

Use the word cards on Unit 31 Resource 1: Too many twos to remember! to recap the spellings of these words. Use the cards to play a game of pairs.

Ask these children to work in pairs to create a short sketch for one of the words (not all will be very easy). As the children present the sketch, the other children must guess the word and say the spelling, using one of the word cards if they like.

Embed

List the homophones covered in this unit and ask the children to tell you which they find hardest. Ask them to spend a few minutes with a partner thinking up as many sentences as possible for this homophone to try and embed it in their mind. Explain that the word 'too' is frequently misspelt, even by adults. Recommend that they pause every time they write the word 'to', 'too' or 'two' and double-check the spelling.

Ask the children to complete Unit 31 Resource 2: Definition mission. (**Answers** knight – a soldier on horseback from a long time ago, night – the opposite of day, too – also or very, two – the number 2, won – the past tense of 'win', bee – a small, stripy, furry insect that makes honey, one – the number 1)

Challenge

Provide these children with a further set of homophones to investigate and learn: 'sum'/'some', 'ate'/'eight', 'been'/'bean', 'cheep'/'cheap'.

Homework / Additional activities

Spelling test

Ask the children to learn the following sentences:

It's good to be green and recycle.

A bee landed on the cake and we all screamed.

The old knight put down his sword.

At night, fairies dance in the garden.

It is two days until my birthday.

We are going to visit Auntie Jo.

I am too ill to go to school.

Can I have one more sweet, please?

Suzy ran fast and won the race.

Collins Connect: Unit 31

Ask the children to complete Unit 31 (see Teach → Year 2 → Spelling → Unit 31).

Note: the Collins Connect activities could be used with Units 29–31.

Review unit 3

A. Children look at the groups of words. They cross out the word with the spelling mistake in each group, then write the correct spelling.

1. ~~wor~~ war [example]

2. ~~werst~~ worst [1 mark]

3. ~~uzual~~ usual [1 mark]

4. ~~meazure~~ measure [1 mark]

5. ~~easilly~~ easily [1 mark]

B. Children add the endings shown to the words. They write the new word. Remind them that they might need to change some letters.

1. *noisily* [example]

2. movement [1 mark]

3. happiness [1 mark]

4. easily [1 mark]

5. harmless [1 mark]

C. Children write the phrases using contractions.

1. *I'm* [example]

2. wasn't [1 mark]

3. she's [1 mark]

4. they'll [1 mark]

5. we'll [1 mark]

D. Children look at the phrases, which are all missing an apostrophe. They write out the phrase, putting in the missing apostrophe.

1. *Jana's coming to tea.* [example]

2. There's my bag! [1 mark]

3. Find Chloe's shoes. [1 mark]

4. The chair's legs are wobbly. [1 mark]

E. Children copy and complete the sentences, choosing the correct spelling from the brackets.

1. *Please pour me a cup of tea.* [example]

2. Can you hear me talking to you? [1 mark]

3. Hooray – they're coming now! [1 mark]

4. My train arrives at the station at 2 o'clock. [1 mark]

5. The directions say we should go left here. [1 mark]

Sort it out

Cut out these words. Read each word with a partner. Sort the words into those that have the **/j/** sound and those that don't.

Sort the words that have the **/j/** sound into those with the **j** spelling and those with the **–ge** spelling.

huge	John	jam
join	large	pig
wag	jump	stage
log	wage	change
joy	hug	jog
peg	sage	charge

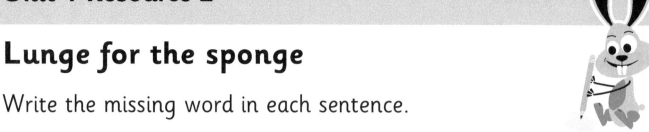

Lunge for the sponge

Write the missing word in each sentence.

1. We went to ch_____ our library books.

2. There was a h_____ present under the tree.

3. The last p_____ of the book was missing.

4. My favourite colour is o_____.

5. The singers stood on the st_____ ready to sing.

6. Max used a sp_____ to clean up the spilt milk.

Can you sort out these muddled words to make words ending in **–ge**?

a g w e _____

g a e _____

r a g e l _____

g a e p _____

Circle time

Sort these words into the correct circle.

Underline words with a long vowel sound. Can you see a pattern?

wage	bridge	stage	fudge	judge	huge
badge	cage	range	sledge	edge	fridge

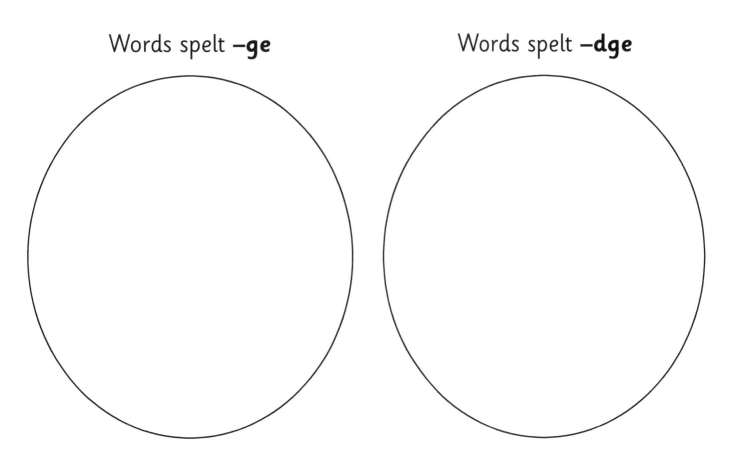

Words spelt **–ge**

Words spelt **–dge**

Bage or badge?

Choose **–ge** or **–dge** to complete the missing words in these sentences.

1. The blackbird made a nest in the he_____.

2. Petra and Matt zoomed down the slope on their sle_____.

3. Marek bought a bag of fu_____ and a bar of chocolate.

4. Sadly, cabba_____ and peas are healthier than cake and ice cream.

5. Granny sent Polly a packa_____ in the post.

6. Shazia put the milk in the fri_____.

7. The hu_____ bear stood up and growled.

8. We need flour, milk and three lar_____ eggs.

Rice and mice

Read these words. Write them in the correct cloud.

Look at the letter after the letter **s** or **c**. What do you notice?

city   police   books   circle   sat   pace   list   prince   mice
France   icy   sung   snip   swim   cygnet   pencil   centre   rice

The /s/ sound spelt **s**

The /s/ sound spelt **c**

Spelling spotter

Choose the correct spelling of these words.
Cross out the spelling that is wrong.

fansy / fancy	sing / cing

centre / sentre

danse / dance	chase / chace

pease / peace

juice / juise	mice / mise

sircle / circle

chanse / chance	pensil / pencil

voise / voice

city / sity	bouncy / bounsy

bicycle / bisycle

Four in a row

Look for words beginning **kn–**. Can you find four
in a row?

knock	knee	knit	know	never	knight
no	name	nice	knife	nugget	knew
now	nine	not	knight	near	know
knot	knew	knives	knob	new	knit
nip	neck	none	nut	nasty	nappy
night	north	knuckles	knelt	knobbly	knotted

Do you know which no?

Complete these sentences by choosing the correct word.

1. I _____ a girl called Susie.   (no / know)

2. Why are there _____ cakes left?   (no / know)

3. Sorry, I don't _____ where he is.   (no / know)

4. Do you _____ if we are doing PE?   (no / know)

5. Can you help me? I'm _____ here.   (new / knew)

6. Ezra _____ it was going to be a good day.
    (new / knew)

7. Well done! I _____ you were going to win.
    (new / knew)

8. It was a dark and stormy _____.   (night / knight)

9. The brave _____ glared at the dragon.
    (night / knight)

Write and wrong

Choose the correct word to complete the sentence.

1. No, that is the _____ answer.   (wrong / rong)

2. Don't pick up the _____ shoes.   (wrong / rong)

3. Yes, that is the _____ book.   (write / right)

4. Turn _____ at the end of the road.   (write / right)

5. _____ your name at the top of the page.

(write / right)

6. It is _____ to throw sand.   (wrong / rong)

7. Freya _____ a thank you letter.   (wrote / rote)

8. We are going to _____ our stories tomorrow.

(write / right)

Wriggles and wrinkles

Colour in the words that are spelt correctly.
Cross out those that are not.

wrong	wrinkle	ren
wrote	wriggle	right
read	wrapped	riggle
reck	wreck	wrapper
risked	write	rist
roat	wrap	wristband
rong	rinkle	wrist

Apple on the table

Can you split these words up into their different sounds? Remember, some sounds will be written using two letters. The first one has been done for you.

1. middle

m	i	dd	le

2. purple

3. apple

4. table

5. circle

6. jingle

7. pimple

8. stubble

At the fair

Can you find all the items in this picture that are spelt **-le** at the end? There are 15 items. Try to find at least 10 of them.

Word match

Draw lines to connect each word to the correct picture.

camel

vowels

jewel

squirrel

towel

kennel

tunnel

parcel

a e i

o u

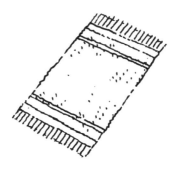

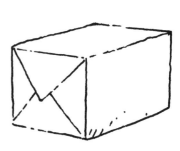

Choosing –le and –el

Can you remember which words end **–le** and which end **–el**? Choose the correct spelling to complete each sentence.

1. Tobie took the _____ to the post office.   (parcle / parcel)

2. Oliver sat in the _____ of the circle.   (middle / middel)

3. The boys had a _____ about the toy.   (quarrle / quarrel)

4. Tigers live in the _____.   (jungle / jungel)

5. Mr Shah likes to _____ to hot places.   (travle / travel)

6. Marnie can _____ to school.   (cycle / cycel)

7. I think cabbage is _____.   (horribel / horrible)

8. The _____ is very posh.   (hotle / hotel)

Green crystal

Colour in the boxes with the words that end **–le** in yellow, the words that end **–el** in red and the words that end **–al** in green.

towel	general	squirrel	vowel
digital	animal	natural	purple
possible	jiggle	wobble	hospital
panel	total	jewel	circle
cable	canal	final	tunnel
crystal	signal	simple	camel

Spelling trios

Choose the correct spelling for each of these words.

towle	towel	towal
digitle	digitel	digital
possible	possibel	possibal
generle	generel	general
camle	camel	camal
jiggle	jiggel	jiggal
squirrle	squirrel	squirral
naturle	naturel	natural
wobble	wobbel	wobbal
vowle	vowel	vowal
purple	purpel	purpal
hospitle	hospitel	hospital

Fossil, gerbil, basil

Write the word under the picture.

| pencil | nostril | gerbil | until | pupil | basil | fossil |

_____

_____

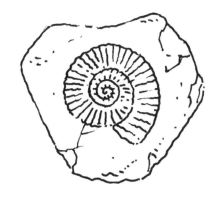

_____

_____

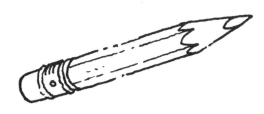

_____

_____

Memory test

Can you remember these words? Test your partner. Give your partner two minutes to look at this sheet then see how many they can remember. Tick them off as they say each word.

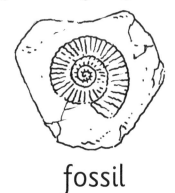

fossil

pupil

peril

gerbil

tonsil

nostril

stencil

Brazil

basil

daffodil

April

pencil

Lock and key

Which lock does the key fit? Follow the words where **/igh/** is spelt **–y** to find out. (Draw a line to join the words to find the path.)

crime	light	find	rise	dries	hide	slide	pie
sigh	cries	shy	chime	ties	line	cries	fight
pie	my	wife	deny	shies	pine	bite	lie
spy	knight	shine	pile	try	kite	flight	untie
smile	night	sigh	invite	hike	cry	high	ice
I	line	untie	stripe	fright	mine	fry	find
wire	thigh	dive	wild	bike	time	flies	dry

Crossword

Complete the crossword. Hint: all the words have an **/igh/** sound spelt **–y**.

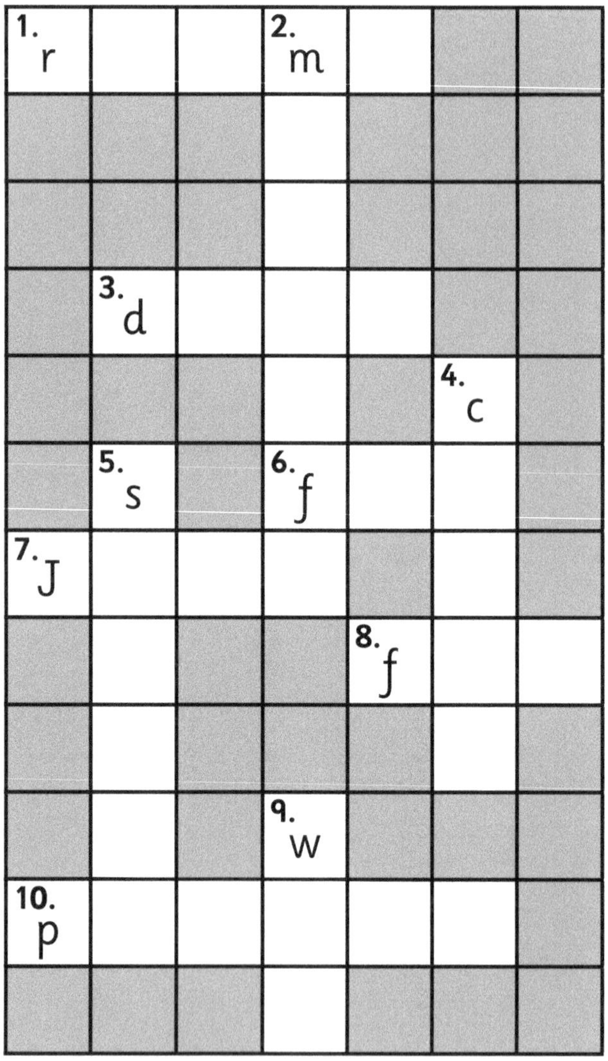

Across

1. To have the same sound at the end. Used in poetry.

3. To say that something isn't true.

6. To cook in a frying pan.

7. The seventh month of the year.

8. A small black insect with wings.

10. A snake that lives in the rainforest and squeezes its prey to death.

Down

2. To make larger.

4. To go somewhere on a bicycle.

5. To give someone something they needed.

9. A questions that sounds like 'Y'.

Try to complete the crossword with these words hidden. Only unfold the bottom of the page when you are really stuck.

- -

The crossword answers are among these words.

cry   why   sky   dry   shy   July   try   sty   deny   supply   fly
rely   magnify   identify   rhyme   python   cycle   fry

Rule spotter

1. Circle the words that you need to change when adding **–s**.

light

berry

bag

lorry

chair

hobby

hurry

sing

2. Write the new words.

one buggy → two _____

one army → two _____

I marry → he _____

I worry → she _____

One welly, two wellies

1. Create the plural for these nouns.

one welly → two _____

one bag → two _____

one army → two _____

one hobby → two _____

one sunrise → two _____

one buggy → two _____

one jeep → two _____

one diary → two _____

one story→ two _____

one surprise→ two _____

one bicycle → two _____

2. Create the third person verbs.

I marry → he _____

We worry → she _____

I empty → it _____

We think → she _____

They sing→ he _____

You supply → she _____

I carry → he _____

Hurried word cards

Cut out the cards below. Use them to create the following words:

carry → carried → carries

copy → copies → copied

worry → worried → worries

study → studied → studies

fancied → fancies → fancy

hurry → hurried → hurries

fried → fry → fries

carr	y	i	es	ed
cop	y	i	es	ed
worr	y	i	es	ed
stud	y	i	es	ed
fanc	y	i	es	ed
hurr	y	i	es	ed
fr	y	i	es	ed

A hurried word search

Can you find the following words in this word search?

copied	hurried	worried	studied	carried
tried	married	tidied	replied	emptied

t	i	d	i	e	d	c	h	j	e	w	m
a	n	y	t	l	p	z	o	p	w	o	a
z	y	e	m	p	t	i	e	d	o	e	r
c	o	p	i	e	d	n	c	f	r	q	r
n	w	k	i	p	n	u	a	j	r	f	i
q	c	m	b	s	v	b	r	v	i	j	e
g	f	w	m	t	b	n	r	k	e	z	d
c	x	n	h	u	r	r	i	e	d	k	x
x	k	z	l	d	m	p	e	z	t	e	t
g	h	t	r	i	e	d	d	b	g	z	v
x	u	f	i	e	y	u	j	n	b	l	q
j	q	h	z	d	r	e	p	l	i	e	d

Funnier word cards

Cut out the cards below. Use them to create the following words:

muddy → muddier → muddiest

yucky → yuckier → yuckiest

soggy → soggiest → soggier

jolliest → jolly → jollier

fancier → fanciest → fancy

silliest → sillier → silly

drier → dry → driest

mudd	y	i	er	est
yuck	y	i	er	est
sogg	y	i	er	est
joll	y	i	er	est
fanc	y	i	er	est
sill	y	i	er	est
dr	y	i	er	est

Silliest sentences

Change the adjective to make it fit the sentence.

1. The new boy was wearing the _____ trousers I'd ever seen. (baggy)

2. That is the _____ joke I've ever heard. (silly)

3. Uncle Robert cooked us the _____ meal I've ever eaten. (tasty)

4. Sadly, we chose the _____ staircase for our escape, and he heard us. (creaky)

5. My father has the _____ car of all time. [rusty]

6. Luckily, our trip was on the _____ day of the holidays. (sunny)

Multiply endings

Add the endings and write the new words in the correct circle. Only two words can have **-est** added.

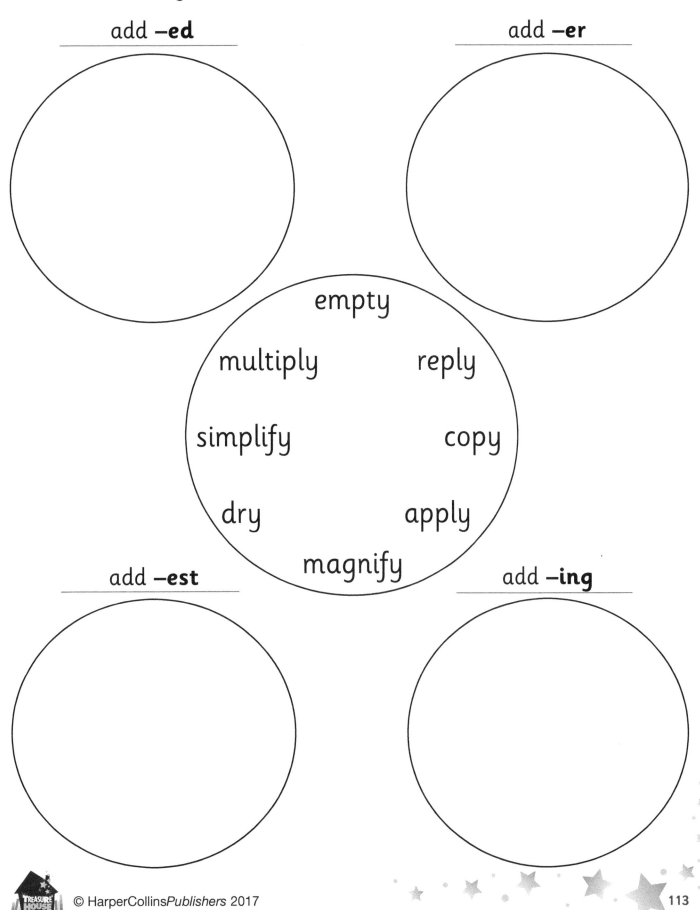

add **-ed**

add **-er**

empty

multiply   reply

simplify   copy

dry   apply

magnify

add **-est**

add **-ing**

Tons of sums

Can you remember whether or not to change the root word when you add **–s**, **–er**, **–est**, **–es** and **–ing**? Complete the word sums.

early + –est _____

busy + –er _____

tiny + –est _____

boy + –s _____

polish + –ing _____

stay + –ing _____

angry + –er _____

bury + –ing _____

easy + –er _____

wealthy + –er _____

story + –es _____

empty + –est _____

Working hard

What jobs do these people have? Add **–er** to the clue word to find out. One has been done for you.

1.

bake <u>baker</u>

2.

tile _____

3.

strike _____

4.

mine _____

5.

write _____

6.

drive _____

7.

care _____

8.

dance _____

Dance, dancer, dancing

Change the given word so that it fits into
the sentence.

1. That dress is too _____ for me. (lace)

2. Sir Brave was the _____ knight in the land.
(brave)

3. Max's baby brother was always _____. (smile)

4. Lilah cried and _____ until we let her play
too. (whine)

5. We _____ so badly at the party, Mum took us
home early. (behave)

6. The playground was _____ and dangerous. (ice)

7. Samia has the world's _____ pet dog. (cute)

8. "You are the _____ child I've ever met," said
Mrs Parker. (rude)

Double letters

Can you split these words up into their different sounds? Remember, some sounds will be written using two letters. Write one sound in each box.

1. run

r	u	n

2. runny

3. dig

4. digger

5. shop

6. shopping

7. clap

8. clapped

Running on a sunny day

Change the given word so that it fits the sentence by adding **-ed**, **-er**, **-ing**, **-est** or **-y**. Write the word in the gap. One has been done for you.

1. Tobias <u>hopped</u> home. (hop)

2. "Stop _____ !" said the teacher. (chat)

3. Please pass me the _____. (rub)

4. It was a lovely _____ day. (sun)

5. It is hard to do up the top _____ on my coat. (pop)

6. Alfie's brother is the _____ boy in the rugby club. (fit)

7. Team A will be _____ first. (bat)

8. Bella _____ the chair nearer the TV. (drag)

Sort them all out

Look at these words. Write the words with **/or/** spelt **al** or **all** in the circles. Cross out the other words.

tap	all	an	ball	hat	talk	tall	can
hall	for	small	walk	call	always	sport	

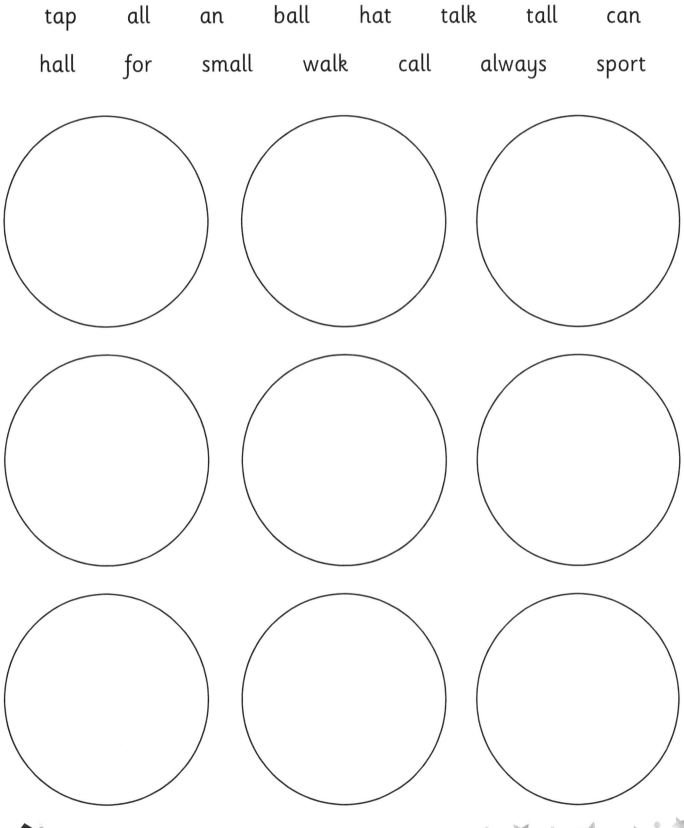

Find them all

Find all the words in this passage that have the **/or/** sound spelt **a** before **l** or **ll**. Write the words you find in the correct bag.

Antonio and his dad sat on the small wall outside Tom's house. They almost always called for Tom on the way to the match and Tom was almost always late. Today, it was already 1pm and Tom wasn't out yet. Still, being a bit late was a small price to pay for the chance to walk to the match with a friend, talking about the players. Sometimes they would also walk with Freddy and his dad who lived next door, but they were often very late if they all walked together.

/or/ spelt **al**

/or/ spelt **all**

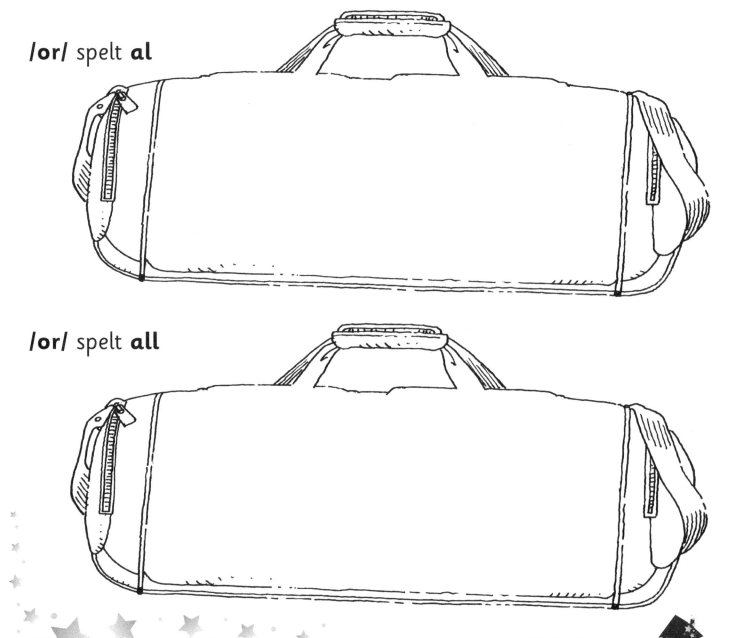

Picture match

Cut out the word cards from the words sheet.

Find the right word card for each picture. Stick the word card next to the picture.

Pairs

Cut out the cards from two copies of this sheet.

Use the cards to play pairs: place all the cards face down and take turns to turn two over. If they are the same, keep the pairs. If they are different, turn them back over. The winner is the person with the most pairs at the end.

brother	love	one
cover	Monday	other
done	month	some
glove	mother	son
honey	money	won

© HarperCollins*Publishers* 2017

Finish it off

Can you finish these words?

1.

Two turk_____

2.

Three curts_____

3.

two troll_____

4.

Which all_____?

5.

Lots of monk_____

6.

A bunch of k_____

Plural mix up

Write the missing word.

1. one turkey,
two _____

2. one journey,
five _____

3. one curtsey,
three _____

4. one trolley,
two _____

5. one jockey,
four _____

6. one alley,
two _____

7. one monkey,
lots of _____

8. He _____ a bunch
of _____. (carry, key)

9. She _____ to the house with

two _____ (hurry, chimney)

Match the word

Write the correct word under each picture.

| wasp | swamp | swan | wallet | watch | wand | wash | squash |

1.

_____

2.

_____

3.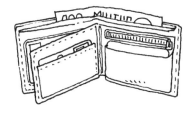

_____

4.

_____

5.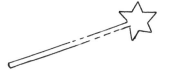

_____

6.

_____

7.

_____

8.

_____

Word duos

Choose words from the box to complete
the sentences.

wasps	swamp	wants	watch	swan	squash

1. There were _____ buzzing around an apple.

2. My father _____ a new car.

3. I saw a _____ glide down the river.

4. I drank a glass of orange _____.

5. A _____ is a wet, muddy place.

6. Tonight I will _____ a play at the theatre.

Write a sentence using 'squabble' and 'quarrel'.

_____

_____

/er/ sound word search

Can you find these words in the word search?
Write the words as you find them.

work   ____ ____ ____ ____

word   ____ ____ ____ ____

worm   ____ ____ ____ ____

world   ____ ____ ____ ____ ____

worse   ____ ____ ____ ____ ____

worst   ____ ____ ____ ____ ____

e	w	o	r	s	t	y	e
p	i	y	g	w	o	r	d
u	w	b	u	o	p	y	i
w	o	r	k	r	e	q	a
g	r	j	z	l	c	z	i
q	s	b	x	d	h	j	x
a	e	e	g	m	u	a	h
q	p	d	c	w	o	r	m

Choose the spelling

Choose the correct spelling of the word to complete the sentence.

1. The television is not _____.
   (working / werking / wurking)

2. _____ right at the end of the street.
   (Torn / Tern / Turn)

3. PE is my _____ lesson.
   (worst / werst / wurst)

4. Kari has very _____ hair.
   (corly / cerly / curly)

5. Mum says I live in a dream _____.
   (world / werld / wurld)

6. Rhythm is a difficult _____ to spell.
   (word / werd / wurd)

Towards awards

Write the missing word. Choose a word from the box.

towards	dwarf	reward	warm	award	warning

1. It was a _____, sunny day.

2. The police offered a _____ for information.

3. 'Danger!' said the _____ sign.

4. Sarah won an _____ for her spelling.

5. The boys raced _____ the finish line.

6. Dopey was Snow White's favourite _____.

Meaning match

Write each word in the box next to its meaning.

war	warm	wardrobe	wart	warn	award	swarm

1. Prize _____

2. Not cold, but not very hot _____

3. Type of lumpy spot _____

4. Cloud of insects _____

5. Series of battles _____

6. Cupboard for clothes _____

7. Alert, caution or threaten _____

A little bit of treasure

Write the word from the box under the correct picture.

| treasure | collision | television | explosion | measure | decision |

1.

2.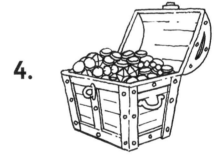

_____

_____

3.

4.

_____

_____

5.

6.

_____

_____

A difficult decision

Complete these words by adding **–sion** or **–sure** to the end.

1. televi_____ _____ _____ _____

2. deci_____ _____ _____ _____

3. mea_____ _____ _____ _____

4. lei_____ _____ _____ _____

5. trea_____ _____ _____ _____

6. explo_____ _____ _____ _____

7. plea_____ _____ _____ _____

8. ver_____ _____ _____ _____

9. occa_____ _____ _____ _____

10. conclu_____ _____ _____ _____

11. confu_____ _____ _____ _____

12. colli_____ _____ _____ _____

Add it on!

Write the word.

real + –ly _____

like + –ly _____

clear + –ly _____

final + –ly _____

quick + –ly _____

use + –ful _____

hope + –ful _____

pain + –ful _____

care + –ful _____

Write the correct spelling.

really / realy _____

lovelly / lovely _____

finally / finaly _____

harmfull / harmful _____

stressfull / stressful _____

fearfull / fearful _____

Hopefully adding helpful suffixes

Add the suffix to the word.

care + –ful		pay + –ment
wonder + –ful		move +– ment
thought + –less		agree + –ment
worth + –less		engage + –ment
time + –less		dark + –ness
fear + –less		thick + –ness
usual + –ly		quick + –ness
clear +– ly		brave + –ness
real + –ly		use + –ful
final + –ly		power + –ful

Lucky and luckily

Can you spell these words? One has been done for you.

lazy + ly   _lazily_

pretty + –ly   _____

nasty + –ly   _____

noisy + –ly   _____

unhappy + –ly   _____

sleepy + –ly   _____

Can you split these words into root plus ending? One has been done for you.

easily   _easy + –ly_

happily   _____

dreamily   _____

naughtily   _____

healthily   _____

Heavily and angrily

Add either **–ment** or **–ly** to these root words. Make sure the word you write is a real word! Don't forget to check if you need to change the **y** to an **i** – you won't always need to.

easy	
enjoy	
heavy	
hasty	
pay	
angry	
merry	

Add either **–ness** or **–less** to these words. Check that the new word makes sense.

greedy	
joy	
lonely	
shy	
penny	
pity	
gooey	
nasty	

Contraction pairs

Cut out these cards and match up the short and long versions.

Muddle up the cards again, turn them over and spread them out. Play a game of 'Pairs' with a partner.

don't	isn't	he's	I'll
you're	can't	didn't	it's
do not	is not	he is	I will
you are	cannot	did not	it is

Pull it together!

Write the contracted versions of these words.

do not		did not	
is not		it is	
he is		they are	
I will		we are	
you are		we would	
cannot		how is	
when will		that is	
where will		they have	

© HarperCollins*Publishers* 2017

Whose arm is this?

Complete each label. One has been done for you.

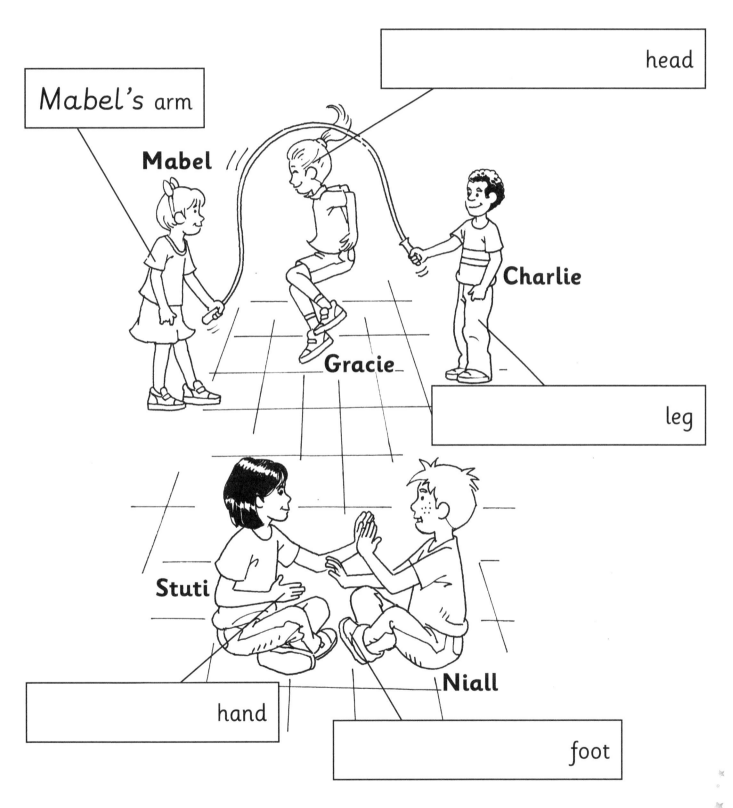

Mabel's arm

head

Mabel

Charlie

Gracie

leg

Stuti

Niall

hand

foot

Wanted: missing apostrophe

Can you add an apostrophe to these sentences to show possession? Watch out: there are two sentences that don't need apostrophes.

1. We rescued the wizards wand from the cave.

2. Tashi and the two Janes found Bernies necklace.

3. The chairs legs are wobbly.

4. The trains whistle is very loud.

5. It's too late to hear everyones poems.

6. Take a large orange and take off its peel.

7. The computers lights are flashing.

8. Look at that bird – I think its wing is broken.

Action at the station

Complete each word by adding **–tion** to the end.
Read the word, then write it out in full.

1. mo____ ____ ____ ____ _____

2. po____ ____ ____ ____ _____

3. ac____ ____ ____ ____ _____

4. sta____ ____ ____ ____ _____

5. ques____ ____ ____ ____ _____

6. direc____ ____ ____ ____ _____

7. men____ ____ ____ ____ _____

8. informa____ ____ ____ ____ _____

Wrong direction

Cut out the words at the bottom and put them
in a (clean) sock. Take turns with a partner to read
a word. If your partner spells the word right he or she
gets to keep it. Who has the most words at the end?

Put the words out of sight and complete the sentences below.

1. We went to the train _____ to pick up Granny.

2. I like to watch the _____ before school.

3. We read the _____ board at the zoo.

4. Who knows the answer to my _____?

5. Telling the truth was the right _____

6. The cars and factories in the area cause _____.

7. The _____ to the maths problem was easy.

8. We went the wrong _____ and got lost.

9. The identical twins in our class cause lots of _____.

question	decision	information	direction	station	solution	television	pollution	confusion

Write it right

Write the words under the picture clues.

Use these picture clues to help you remember the words.

right	write	so	sew	hear	here	whole	hole

1.

_____

2.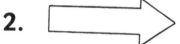

_____

3.

what?

_____

4.

_____

5.

_____

6.

_____

7.

_____

8.

_____

Here, hear!

Cut out these words.

You will need three players. Player 1 says a sentence for each word, emphasising the key word. Players 2 and 3 race to pick up the correct card. The player with the most cards at the end wins. Swap roles at the end of each game.

right	write
so	sew
hear	here
there	their
whole	hole

Pairs of pears

Use these cards to play a game of pairs with a partner.

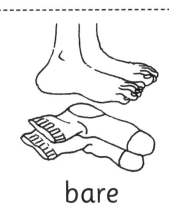

bare

bear

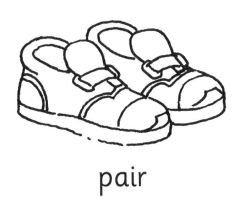

pair

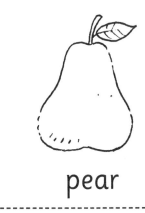

pear

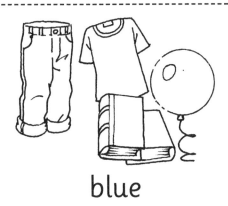

blue

blew

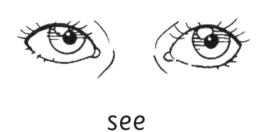

see

sea

Definition match

Draw lines to match the words to their definitions.

blew	to be naked or uncovered
pair	a large furry animal
pear	two items that match or fit together
bare	a type of fruit that grows on a tree
see	the colour of the sky on a sunny day
blue	to look or to spot something
sea	the past tense of 'blow'
bear	the ocean

Too many twos to remember!

Use these cards to play a game of pairs with a partner.

knight

night

too

two

won

one

be

bee

Definition mission

Draw lines to match the words to their definitions.

knight	the opposite of day
night	also or very
too	a small, stripy, furry insect that makes honey
two	a soldier on horseback from a long time ago
won	the number 1
bee	the number 2
one	the past tense of 'win'